Learning Language Arts Through Literature

THE RED
TEACHER BOOK

By

Debbie Strayer

and

Susan Simpson

Common Sense Press

The *Learning Language Arts Through Literature* series:

The Blue Book - 1st Grade Skills
The Red Book - 2nd Grade Skills
The Yellow Book - 3rd Grade Skills
The Orange Book - 4th Grade Skills
The Purple Book - 5th Grade Skills
The Tan Book - 6th Grade Skills
The Green Book - 7th Grade Skills
The Gray Book - 8th Grade Skills
The Gold Book - World Literature - High School Skills
The Gold Book - American Literature - High School Skills
The Gold Book - British Literature - High School Skills

Copyright ©1998 by:
Common Sense Press, Inc.
8786 Highway 21
Melrose, FL 32666
www.commonsensepress.com

Printed in the United States of America.

Rev 07/08
Printed 04/16

ISBN 978-1-880892-82-4

Introduction

Welcome to *Learning Language Arts Through Literature, The Red Book*, which is part of *The Common Sense Reading Program*. It is the perfect follow-up to *The Blue Book*, or it may be used after successfully completing another first grade program.

The Red Book begins with a short review of first grade skills and continues in second grade skills. The easy-to-use format is both understandable for the teacher and enjoyable for the student. Using Dr. Ruth Beechick's principles, this sound and proven method ensures that the necessary grammar and reading skills are taught. Higher-order thinking skills usually overlooked by other programs challenge your student into higher learning.

The Common Sense Reading Program

Foundation

This program provides step-by-step assistance for teachers as they guide their beginning or fluent reader through reading skills. For the beginning reader, *The Red Book* encourages your student in reading skills in an easy and relaxed manner. Your student feels successful and improves his reading skills as the year progresses, learning language arts skills at the same time.

For the fluent reader, *The Red Book* encourages his love of reading. The necessary spelling, grammar, and writing skills are taught using the six readers. In order to determine which skills to present in this program, the authors drew from their own classroom teaching, from experience teaching their own students to read, and from the excellent information obtained from two primary sources: *A Home Start in Reading* by Dr. Ruth Beechick; and *Teaching Students: A Curriculum Guide to What Students Need to Know at Each Level Through Sixth Grade* by Diane Lopez.

Structure

The Red Book portion of *The Common Sense Reading Program* is divided into three parts, a total of 36 lessons. It is expected that each lesson will take one week, thus providing 36 weeks of instruction, which is equivalent to the common 180 day school year.

Each of the 36 weekly lessons is divided into five days. Though this may seem overly structured to some teachers, the purpose is to provide all the support necessary to teach your student successfully. However, feel free to make adjustments as needed to fit this plan of instruction to your particular situation.

Using Real Books for Reading and Language Arts

The Common Sense Reading Program is unique in that the instruction and materials enable your student to read "real" books, rather than a basal-type reader. By purchasing this program, you have obtained six individual real reading books. Your student will enjoy reading these books as he uses them for reading and language arts instruction.

Six readers from the *Successful Reading for Beginners* series are included, each containing five or six stories in each book. They are:
- *All Around the Farm*
- *Forest Fables*
- *In, Out, and About Catfish Pond*
- *Up, Down, and Around the Rain Tree*
- *Underwater Friends*
- *Famous People*

Enrichment Activities

In most of the lessons you will find the treasure chest icon for the *Enrichment Activities*. While optional, these activities develop thinking and reasoning skills necessary for higher level learning. These activities are especially recommended for the fluent reader who may require more challenging activities or independent work.

Assessments

This book provides you with seven *Assessments*, about one every five weeks. Easy-to-use directions help you evaluate your student's progress.

Additional Literature Used in Lessons

At the back of the book, you will find a list of books necessary to complete this program. Favorite classics have been chosen to encourage your student in the joy of reading. They are conveniently listed in the order in which they are introduced in the lessons.

Books from which literature passages have been taken are not required to complete this program.

Student Activity Book

The *Student Activity Book* contains everything he needs to complete the program successfully. Also included are handwriting pages, cut and paste activities, and much more. These are referred to in the lessons, with specific references to make them easy to find.

The binding of the *Student Activity Book* is designed so that the pages are easily removed. Simply grasp the top right corner of a page, and gently pull it out as you would remove a piece of paper from a pad.

The *Student Activity Book's* back cover is a special page for your student. You should cut this off at the line and store it in a safe place. The miniature covers of the readers will be used during the year.

Table of Contents

Introduction to Part 1

These first four weeks are primarily a time of review, although a few new phonics skills are included in the lessons. Most students need this time to refresh their memories and get into the swing of the lessons again. For some students, the phonics instruction may not be necessary, so feel free to use them only as needed.

Throughout the program you are asked to read stories, passages, or activities to or with your student. The material to be read was carefully chosen. Your student will benefit from the lesson activity whether he is a fluent or beginning reader. If he begins to read aloud and has difficulty with a word, simply tell him the word at that time. If you insist that he sound out the word, he will lose the flow of the reading. Make a note that he needs instruction on the sounds in that word and work on it later. When your student reads aloud, it is best to make it a successful and enjoyable experience.

Included in the lessons are *Enrichment Activities* to expand your student's thinking, reasoning, and writing skills. These activities are excellent for the fluent reader who is not completing the phonics lessons. They will be beneficial for the nonreading student as well. Ask him to dictate his thoughts to you as you write them down. Please use these activities as you desire.

Specific *Spelling* and *Handwriting* instruction begins in Lesson 5. During these first lessons, your student will be involved in plenty of activities that will strengthen these skills as well as prepare him for the more structured lessons to come.

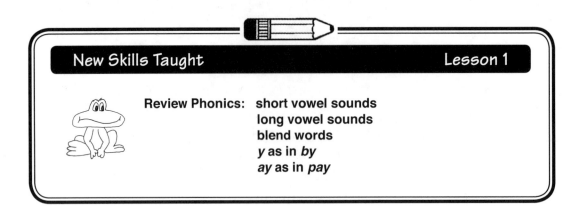

Review Phonics: short vowel sounds
long vowel sounds
blend words
y as in *by*
ay as in *pay*

✏ **Teacher's Note:**
Remember to make reading aloud a successful event for your student.

Materials needed:
A Tree Is Nice by Janice May Udry

Day 1

a. Read the following literature passage to your student. Ask your student to follow you in the *Student Activity Book*.

> *Come over to my house,*
> *I live in a boat.*
> *I live in a city*
> *of houses that float.*
>
> *Come into my houseboat.*
> *Have supper with me.*
> *I'll give you cold rice*
> *and a cup of hot tea.*

b. Talk with your student about the poem. You may use the following questions to help you in your discussion.

1) *Do you know anyone who lives in a boat?*
2) *People from different countries live in different kinds of houses. In what country do you think this person lives?*
3) *Children from different countries are different in many ways. All children want friends to "come over to my house." Who do you invite to your house?*
4) *No matter where we live, a home is where we live with the people whom we love. What makes your home special?*

c. Look at the first line of the poem. Read the line to your student, or your student may read it to you. Point to the word *house*, and ask him to underline it. Tell him that the word *house* is a naming word. A naming word names a person, place, or thing. The word *house* names a thing.

Look at the second line of the poem. Read the line to your student, or your student may read it to you. Ask your student to find the naming word and underline it. **boat** Ask your student to find the naming word in the third line and underline it. **city** The fourth line. **houses**

 d. Ask your student to read the Short Vowel Words.

sat	hot	cup	lip	run	fed
tin	bog	pet	log	mad	ax
zip	jug	tax	gas	yak	van
quit	quiz	wit	kin	rob	dam

e. Ask your student to look at the picture. Tell him to read each sentence and place an X beside the sentence which best describes the picture.

  __ 1) Tim is mad.   **X** 2) Tim is sad.
  __ 3) Tim is on a mat.   ___ 4) Tim will run.

 Ask your student to write or dictate a sentence about the picture.

f. Read the words in the Phonics Word Box and ask your student to choose one to complete the sentences: *run hot cup sat bit*.

  1) The man **sat** on the box.
  2) The sun is **hot**.
  3) The dog **bit** him.
  4) He will hop, and I will **run**.
  5) A mug is a **cup**.

Using a separate piece of paper, illustrate two of the sentences above. Your student may copy the sentences under the illustrations.

g. Find page 5 in the *Student Activity Book*. Ask your student to cut out all the picture and word cards. Place the picture cards side by side. Ask your student to read each word and place it under the picture card that uses the same vowel sound. After this is completed, ask your student to read the words in each row. Store the cards in separate envelopes according to vowel sounds.

ă   **apple - sat, ham, nap, yam, cat, lad, bag, dad**
ĕ   **elephant - met, leg, ten, hen, bed, web, set, peg**
ĭ   **igloo - pig, bib, lid, rib, hit, tin, big, win**
ŏ   **octopus - hot, rob, top, not, log, mom, dog, job**
ŭ   **umbrella - cub, mud, bus, rub, nut, sun, tug, fun**

h. Find page 3 in the *Student Activity Book*. Just like in the poem, your student can invite friends to his house. Ask your student to cut along the lines and fold forward. Ask him to write his name on the front, and then draw pictures of his friends inside his house. Ask him to write their names underneath. Help him with any spelling.

Day 2

a. Read the literature passage from *Come Over to My House* again, or your student may read it to you.

b. The literature passage refers to *cold rice* and *hot tea*. Ask your student what he notices about the words *cold* and *hot*. Words like *cold* and *hot* have opposite meanings. These words are called **antonyms**.

Ask your student to look at the first verse of the literature passage as you read it again. Which word has an opposite meaning of *go*? Circle the word. **come** Which word has an opposite meaning of *sink*? Circle the word. **float**

c. Tell your student the following rule to help him remember how to read some words:

When two vowels go walking, the first one usually does the talking and says his long name.

d. Ask your student to look at the picture. Tell your student to read each sentence and place an X beside the sentence which best describes the picture.

__ 1) I can bake a cake. __ 2) I like to hike.
__ 3) I can win a race.   **X** 4) I can rake.

Ask your student to write or dictate a sentence about the picture.

4

e. Find page 9 in the *Student Activity Book*. Ask your student to cut out all the picture and word cards. Place the picture cards side by side. Ask your student to read each word card and place it under the picture that uses the same vowel sound. After this is completed, ask your student to read the words in each row. Store the cards in separate envelopes according to vowel sounds.

ā rake - bake, same, game, tame, make, made, late
ī bike - rise, mine, ride, dime, wise, like, nine
ō rose - nose, home, dome, bone, vote, cone, note
ū ruler - fuse, tube, duke, tune, rule, rude, mule

f. Read the words to or with your student found in the Phonics Word Box in his *Student Activity Book*: *home, tune, kite, rose, bone*. Ask your student to choose a word from the Phonics Word Box to complete these sentences.

1) Nate tore his **kite**.   2) Jake will hum a **tune**.   3) Duke will run **home**.
4) I can smell a **rose**.   5) The dog will hide his **bone**.

 Illustrate any two sentences above on a separate piece of paper.

g. Read the review sight words to your student: *was   were   when   wants*.

The following sentences contain the review sight words. Ask your student to read the sentences to you.

1) *When* will Jake make his kite?
2) He *wants* to make it nice.
3) I was sad when Jake *was* not here.
4) Jake and I *were* pals.

h. Tell your student that countries have different houses, often depending on the materials available and the type of climate. Ask your student to draw, on a separate sheet of paper, the type of house the literature passage describes or any other type of house he is familiar with. Suggestions: igloo, teepee, log cabin, apartment buildings, grass huts, etc. Ask him to write or dictate two sentences to you about the house he drew.

Day 3

a. Read the literature passage to your student.

> *In a faraway place,*
> *in a wide empty land,*
> *my house is a tent*
> *in the wind and the sand.*

Come Over to My House by Theodore LeSeig.
Copyright © 1966 by Random House, Inc.
Reprinted by permission of Random House, Inc.

b. Talk with your student about this verse. You may use the following questions to help you in your discussion.

1) *This verse describes a sandy place in a wide empty land. Where do you think this house is?* **desert**
2) *Do you think the tent is the same kind of tent you sleep in when you go camping?* **No** *How is it different?*
3) *Why do you think these people live in tents?* **They travel from place to place.**

c. Tell your student that sometimes two words are joined together to make a new word. Point to the word *faraway*, and ask your student to underline it. Tell your student that this word is made up of two words. Ask him if he knows what two words make up *faraway*. ***far* and *away*** This is called a compound word.

Show your student the literature passage in **1a**. Ask him if he can find the compound word as you read the passage. Underline the word. **houseboat** What two words make up this compound word? ***house* and *boat***

d. A naming word names a person, place, or thing. Ask your student to circle all the naming words in today's literature passage. Read the literature passage as he circles the words. **place, land, house, tent, wind, sand**

e. If needed, review the following phonics rules:

1) **y** at the end of a short word usually says /ī/ as in *my*
2) **e, i**, and **o** at the end of a short word usually says its long name as in *be, hi, go*
   Teacher's Note: The word *do* is an exception to this rule and therefore is a sight word.
3) **ay** at the end of a word says /ā/ as in *pay*

f. Ask your student to read the Long Vowel Words.

paid	boat	seat	stay	beet
my	ray	try	he	so

g. Ask your student to look at the picture and tell him to place an X beside the sentence which best describes the picture.

___ 1) I like my tie.   ___2) It is a nice day.

__X__ 3) I see a boat.   ___4) I play in the rain.

Ask your student to write or dictate a sentence about the picture using two naming words.

h. Ask your student to read the words in the Phonics Word Box: *boat, team, tail, pie, fly.*

Complete the sentences:
1) The dog plays with his **tail**.
2) Jean plays on a **team**.
3) Fay hopes to go on a **boat**.
4) Luke bakes a **pie**.
5) See the kite **fly**.

Illustrate two of the sentences.

i. Talk about the picture on page 13 of the *Student Activity Book* with your student. You may use the following questions to help you in your discussion. Ask your student to color the picture.

1) *How is this desert family like your family?* **Answers will vary.**
2) *How is this desert family different from your family?*

Day 4

a. Read the book, *A Tree is Nice*, by Janice May Udry to your student. Talk with your student about the story. You may use the following questions to help you in your discussion.

1) *Tell me some of the ways trees are used.*
2) *Do you like trees? What do you like about trees?*
3) *Look at the pictures again and tell me your favorite picture. Why?*
4) *Would you like to plant a tree?*

b. The title of the book is *A Tree is Nice*. What word describes the tree? Underline this word. **nice** The word *nice* is a describing word. There are other ways to describe a tree: green tree, tall tree, old tree, beautiful tree, and so on.

c. Ask your student to think of other words to describe a *tree*. Write the words under the tree on page 14 of the *Student Activity Book* for your student, or he may write it himself with your help. He may color the tree.

Possible answers: big, little, pretty, colorful, brown, shady, etc.

 d. Ask your student to read the Blend Words.

church	ship	smile	track
brick	shy	smog	chase
smell	chime	bride	try

e. Ask your student to look at the picture. Tell your student to read each sentence and place an X beside the sentence which best describes the picture.

___ 1) Brad will go to church.   **X** 2) Chad will sail on a ship.
___ 3) Dale is on the train.   ___ 4) Buck will smile at his bride.

Ask your student to write a sentence about the picture using a describing word.

f. Go outside and ask your student to pick a few leaves he likes. Tell him he will make a leaf rubbing. Place the leaf between two pieces of paper and paper clip along the corners and edges. Remove the crayon wrapping and lay the crayon on its side. Show him how to rub the crayon on the paper covering the leaf. Do it lightly enough not to move the leaf about, but hard enough to make a rubbing. It may take a couple of tries before he does one he is satisfied with.

After your student has completed his leaf rubbing, display his work and allow him to talk about his design.

Variations: Try using more than one color in a single leaf rubbing. Try placing more than one leaf between the sheets. The leaves may be placed randomly or in a specific design.

Day 5

a. Read *A Tree is Nice* to your student again, or ask him to tell you the story in his own words using the pictures if needed.

b. Ask your student to read this paragraph.

It is a fine day. I see the green grass and the clear sky. My black dog runs to five men. The men play with the nice dog. My dog wants to play and play.

c. Remind your student that a naming word names a person, place, or thing. Ask him to underline all the naming words in the above paragraph. **day, grass, sky, dog, men**

d. Ask your student to cut out the word cards for **5d** on page 17 of the *Student Activity Book* and find all the naming words from the above passage. Ask him to fold a piece of paper in half lengthwise and glue the word cards in the right-hand column.

e. Now, ask your student to read the paragraph again. Ask him to find the words that describe each naming word and glue those beside the naming word in the left-hand column. Tell your student that one of the naming words will have two describing words.

fine day	**clear sky**	**five men**
green grass	**nice, black dog**	

f. Ask your student to read the Blend Words:

grass	plum	crab	bless	cram	cry
spy	pluck	grade	blot	speak	stop

g. Ask your student to look at the picture. Tell your student to read each sentence and place an X beside the sentence which best describes the picture.

__1) Glen rode his black bike.   __2) Jill sat on the grass.
__3) Sam will chase a crab.   **X** 4) Stan spoke to his pal.

Ask your student to write or dictate a sentence about the picture using a describing word.

h. Read the review sight words to your student: *come   from   good   happy*.

The following sentences contain the review sight words. Ask your student to read them to you.

1) Chad, *come* sit with me on the grass.   2) Brad will be *happy* to see us.
3) We are *good* pals.   4) The note is *from* Stan.

i. Tell your student that if he looks closely at a tree, he will see branches that spread out from the trunk. We can draw a picture to show how our family is like a tree. Help your student complete the family tree by writing the family members' names. Optional: On a separate piece of paper, make a family tree with pictures from photographs and glue them on the appropriate places. Or, your student may choose to draw the pictures. If more branches are needed for siblings, aunts, and uncles, etc., add more lines and boxes accordingly.

j. Find page 17 in the *Student Activity Book*. Ask your student to cut out the six sections of words for **5j**. Cut out the four words from one section and review with your student how to put them in alphabetical order. To put words in alphabetical order, look at the first letter of each word. Using the first letter of each word, put the words in the same order as the alphabet. Ask your student to do one section of words at a time, being sure not to mix with another section. Keep the word cards in different envelopes or paper clip them together.

ape	bag	big	fit	red	cap
bug	him	fat	get	sat	lap
cap	pop	met	hot	top	nap
dog	rat	sun	is	us	sap

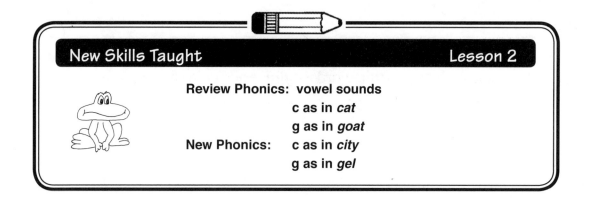

Review Phonics: vowel sounds
c as in *cat*
g as in *goat*
New Phonics: c as in *city*
g as in *gel*

Day 1

a. Find the Story Folder, "David and Goliath," in the *Student Activity Book* page 21. Read it to your student.

b. Talk with your student about the story. You may use the following questions to help you in your discussion.

   1) *Tell me some things that you think David learned while tending his father's sheep.*
   2) *David was just a young boy, but he wanted to fight the biggest, fiercest warrior. Why?*
   3) *It is normal to be afraid of things. What are some things you are afraid of? What can you learn from David about your fears?*

c. Remind your student that a naming word names a person, place, or thing. These naming words are called **nouns**. The word *boy* is a noun because it names a person. It is a **common noun** because it names any boy. In the story we just read, tell me the name of the young shepherd boy. **David**

d. Tell your student that the word *David* is the name of a particular boy. The name of a particular person, place, or thing is called a **proper noun**. A proper noun always begins with a capital letter. Tell your student to write the word *David* under the correct picture. Remind him to begin the name with a capital letter.

Ask your student if he can tell you the name of the "biggest, strongest warrior" whom David fought. **Goliath** Ask him to copy the name under the correct picture. Begin the name with a capital letter. Tell him that the word *Goliath* is a proper noun.

✏ Teacher's Note: The Story Folders are found in the *Student Activity Book*. After you cut it out, fold it to look like a small book.

Day 1. b. Possible answers:
1) He learned about God. He learned to trust Him.
2) He believed that God would win the battle.
3) Answers will vary.

✏ Teacher's Note: *Cannot* may be spelled *cannot* or *can not*. Both ways have been used in this program.

e. Ask your student to listen to this word as you read it aloud: *day*. Ask him to repeat the word and clap for each unbroken sound, or syllable, he hears. Ask your student to repeat the following words after you, clapping hands for each syllable: *sheep   gaze   big   help   sword*.

Ask him to write the number of syllables next to each word on page 20 of the *Student Activity Book*.

All the words are one syllable, so clap only once.

Tell your student that words with one vowel sound usually have one syllable, or sound, in them.

f. Ask your student to listen to this word as you read it aloud: *David*. Ask him to repeat the word and clap for each unbroken sound, or syllable, he hears. Ask your student to repeat the following words after you, or your student may read the words to you. Ask him to clap his hands for each syllable sound he hears: *father   brothers   giant   battle   afraid*.

Ask him to write the number of syllables next to each word.

All the words are two syllables, so clap twice.

g. Ask your student to listen to this word as you read it aloud: *Goliath*. Ask him to repeat the word and clap for each unbroken sound, or syllable he hears. Ask your student to repeat the following words after you, or your student may read the words to you. Ask him to clap his hands for each syllable sound he hears: *warrior   perfectly   permission   victory*.

Ask him to write the number of syllables next to each word.

All the words are three syllables, so clap three times.

h. After the concept of clapping for each sound is understood, mix up the words on your syllable list. Call out the words in random order and ask your student to clap for each syllable while repeating the word.

i. Find pages 23 and 25 in the *Student Activity Book*. Ask your student to make the Word Family Flip Books. Read each word to or with your student.

staple	_ink pl	_ink dr	_ink s	_ink th
	_ink w	_ink cl	_ink bl	_ink m
	_ink p	_ink st	staple	ink

staple	_and st	_and s	_ust m	_ust j
	_and l	_and gr	_ust tr	_ust cr
	_and h	_and b	_ust d	_ust b
	_and br		_ust r	
staple and		staple ust		

plink	sink	wink	stand	land	hand	must	just	trust
pink	drink	blink	brand	sand	grand	crust	dust	bust
clink	mink	think	band			rust		
stink								

j. Ask your student what he notices about each word family. If he doesn't know, tell him that all the words in each word family have the same ending sound. Words with the same ending sound are rhyming words. Poetry often uses rhyme. In Lesson 1, *Come Over to My House* uses rhyme.

Ask your student to choose words from Word Family 1 (**-ink**) to complete this rhyme.
Cups of water in the sink
Thirsty children come to **drink**.

Choose words from Word Family 2 (**-and**) to complete this rhyme.
Land ahoy, I see land,
Let me out to play in the **sand**.

Choose words from Word Family 3 (**-ust**) to complete this rhyme.
I clean and dust,
Mother says I **must**.

k. Tell your student to choose one of the rhymes and draw a picture for it.

l. To put words in alphabetical order, look at the first letter of each word. Using the first letter of each word, put the words in the same order as the alphabet. List the words in Word Family 3 (**-ust**) in alphabetical order.

bust, crust, dust, just, must, rust, trust

Day 2

a. Read the Bible passage from I Samuel 17:4-11 to your student.

>   *A champion named Goliath, who was from Gath, came out of the Philistine camp. He was over nine feet tall. He had a bronze helmet on his head and wore a coat of scale armor of bronze weighing five thousand shekels; on his legs he wore bronze greaves, and a bronze javelin was slung on his back. His spear shaft was like a weaver's rod, and its iron point weighed six hundred shekels. His shield bearer went ahead of him.*
>
>   *Goliath stood and shouted to the ranks of Israel, "Why do you come out and line up for battle? Am I not a Philistine, and are you not the servants of Saul? Choose a man and have him come down to me. If he is able to fight and kill me, we will become your subjects; but if I overcome him and kill him, you will become our subjects and serve us." Then the Philistine said, "This day I defy the ranks of Israel! Give me a man and let us fight each other." On hearing the Philistine's words, Saul and all the Israelites were dismayed and terrified.*

b. Remind your student that a word that names a person, place, or thing is called a noun. The word *city* is a noun. This is called a common noun because there are many cities. The word *Austin* is the name of a particular city. This is called a proper noun.

   Looking at the Bible passage with your student, point out the word *Gath*. Ask him to underline it. Read the word in its context. Ask him if he can tell you why *Gath* begins with a capital letter. **name of a particular place**

   Tell your student to write the name of the city in which he lives. Help him spell the name.

c. Read the first two sentences of the Bible passage again. Ask your student to look at the second sentence. Show him the word *he*, and ask him to circle it. Ask him if he knows for which word *he* replaces. **Goliath** Ask him to underline the word. Tell your student that *he* takes the place of the naming word, Goliath. A word that take the place of a naming word is called a pronoun.

d. Ask your student to look at the first paragraph of the Story Folder, "David and Goliath." Ask him to circle the word *he* every time it is used in the first paragraph.

e. Tell your student that you will read the paragraph again, using the word *David* instead of *he*.

> *David was the youngest of seven brothers. Each brother had a job. David's job was to look after his father's sheep. David did the job well. David learned about God as David worked in the fields. David would gaze at the stars at night and sing songs to God. David trusted God to help him.*

Ask your student which way sounds better to him. Tell him that because it is awkward to use a naming word each time, we use pronouns.

f. Find pages 31 and 33 in the *Student Activity Book*. Ask your student to cut out the Bingo cards and word cards. Shuffle the word cards and take turns drawing cards. As each player draws a card, he reads the word and tells what vowel sound it has. Using any object, such as pennies or beans, all players cover the vowel sound used in that word.

When someone has Bingo, four in a row — vertically, horizontally, or diagonally, he calls out, "Bingo." One of the other players checks the cards that have been read, making sure all covered sounds have been called. If a word is read and the vowel sound is unknown, everyone can help. The goal is to reinforce short and long vowel sound recognition. This is not a test.

Variation: You may keep playing until someone covers the entire card.

g. Ask your student to look at the picture of David and Goliath and color it. Talk to your student about the picture. Ask him if he remembers any details from the story.

 Ask your student to write or dictate two sentences about the picture.

Day 3

a. Read the Bible passage from I Samuel 17:33-37 to your student.

Saul replied, "You are not able to go out against this Philistine and fight him; you are only a boy, and he has been fighting from his youth."

But David said to Saul, "Your servant has been keeping his father's sheep. When a lion or a bear came and carried a sheep from the flock, I went after it, struck it, and rescued the sheep from its mouth. When it turned on me, I seized it by its hair, struck it, and killed it. Your servant has killed both lion and bear; this uncircumcised Philistine will be like one of them, because he has defied the armies of the living God. The Lord who delivered me from the paw of the lion and the paw of the bear will deliver me from the hand of this Philistine."

Saul said to David, "Go, and the Lord be with you."

b. Read these sentences to or with your student.

1) *David was a little boy.*
2) *Did David fight Goliath?*
3) *Yes, he hit the giant right on his head!*

Tell your student that most sentences are telling sentences. Ask him to look at the first sentence. This is a telling sentence and ends with a period. The second sentence asks a question and ends with a question mark. The third sentence shows strong feeling. Sentences like these end with an exclamation mark.

c. Ask your student to read each sentence. Add punctuation to the end of each sentence. Add a period, question mark, or exclamation mark.

1) Will God win for us   **?**
2) David had five stones   **.**
3) When the stone hit Goliath, he fell with a thud   **! or .**
4) God is my help in time of need **! or .**

d. Read the review sight words to your student: *little   look   boy   night.*

The following sentences contain the review sight words. Ask your student to read them to you.

1) David was a *boy*.   2) He liked to *look* at his sheep.
3) At *night* David sang songs.   4) He was *little*, but he had faith in God.

e. A word that takes place of a noun is called a pronoun. Read the sentences to or with your student and ask him to choose the correct pronoun: *We They It She He I*.

1) *Mom is home.*
2) *Dad called us.*
3) *Mom and I like cake.*
4) *Student's name likes pizza.*
5) *The book is fun to read.*
6) *Sam and Pam went home.*

1) **She** is home.
2) **He** called us.
3) **We** like cake.
4) **I** like pizza.
5) **It** is fun to read.
6) **They** went home.

f. Tell your student that the letter **c** can make two different sounds. Listen to the words *cent* and *cane*. They both begin with the same letter, but they do not make the same sound. Ask your student to tell you the two sounds **c** can make. **c says /s/ as in *cent* (soft *c*); c says /k/ as in *cap* (hard *c*)**

Read the list of words to your student, or your student may read them to you. Ask your student to tell you if he hears a hard **c** or a soft **c** after each word: (Example: *cut* **hard c** is circled) *cat* - **hard c**, *city* - **soft c**, *cute* - **hard c**, *cup* - **hard c**, *cent* - **soft wc**, *cereal* - **soft c**, *coat* - **hard c**.

g. Find page 37 in the *Student Activity Book*. Ask your student to cut out the two picture cards and all the word cards. Place the *Hard C Card* and the *Soft C Card* side by side to make two columns. Ask your student to line up the word cards below the correct *C Sound Card*.
Hard C- cap can't cute come cup call
Soft C - cent circle circus center cereal city

After your student has completed the exercise, ask him if he notices any pattern to which column the word cards are placed. If he doesn't notice, tell him the following rule: *c followed by **e**, **i**, or **y** says /s/; c followed by **a** or **u** says /k/*.

Teacher's Note: There are exceptions to this rule. Your student will learn more soft c words as he learns to read multi-syllable words.

h. Ask your student to complete the Long Vowel Word Search Puzzle. Ask him to read the words he circled: *bake tray sail keep team bike tie mule*.

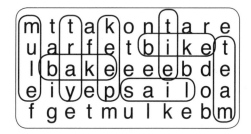

i. Ask your student to tell you orally, in writing, or by illustrating, how God helped David when he was taking care of the sheep.

Day 4

a. Find the Story Folder, "The Country Mouse's Big Adventure," in the *Student Activity Book* page 39. Read it to your student.

b. Talk with your student about the story. You may use the following questions to help you in your discussion.

1) *Tell me two ways the country and city are different, according to our story.*
Possible answers: The country was calm and peaceful. Max's home was a bale of hay in a barn. The house in the city had big rooms. Casey lived with a cat.
2) *What made Max feel safe and content?*
Possible answers: Although Max didn't have a beautiful home, he did not have to fear a cat.

c. Find page 45 in the *Student Activity Book*. Ask your student to cut out the sentence strips for **4c** and put them in the correct order. Optional: He may glue each strip on a piece of paper and illustrate it.

If your student has difficulty with this activity, read two sentences to him and ask which event happened first. Then choose another strip and ask him if it came before or after these events. Continue this process until all the strips are in order.

After you have checked to see if the order is correct, ask him to glue each strip on a piece of paper and illustrate it.

d. Show your student a sentence from the story which uses quotation marks (" "). Tell your student that these marks tell us someone is speaking. The words inside the quotation marks are the spoken words.

Ask your student to look at the story as you read. Use your fingers to show your student where you are reading. Read parts of the story which are enclosed in quotation marks, and parts of the story without quotation marks. Ask your student to tell you if it is a quotation or not.

Ex: "Max, old boy!" - This is a quotation.
His life was calm and quiet, and he liked it that way. - This is not a quotation.

e. Read the review sight words to your student: *they, said, there, very.*

The following sentences contain the review sight words. Ask your student to read them to you.

1) "Come see us," *they* said.   2) The cake was *very* good.
3) "I do not want to go there," he *said.*   4) *They* said, "When can we go?"

f. Tell your student that just like the letter **c**, the letter **g** can make two different sounds. Listen to the words *gum* and *gem*. They both begin with the same letter, but they do not make the same sound. Ask your student to tell you the two sounds **g** can make. **g says /g/ as in *goat* (hard *g*); g says /j/ as in *gem* (soft *g*)**

Ask your student to read the list of words. Ask your student to tell you if he hears a hard **g** or a soft **g** after each word: (Example: *gum* - **hard g** is circled) *goat* - **hard g**, *gas* - **hard g**, *gel* - **soft g**, *gap* - **hard g**, *got* - **hard g**, *gem* - **soft g**.

g. Find page 45 in the *Student Activity Book.* Ask your student to cut out the two picture cards and all the word cards for **4g**. Place the *Hard G Card* and the *Soft G Card* side by side to make two columns. Ask your student to line up the word cards below the correct *G Sound Card.* **Goat - goat gas got gap   Gem - gem gel**

After your student has completed the exercise, ask him if he notices any pattern to which column the word cards are placed. If he doesn't notice, tell him the following rule: **g** followed by **e**, **i**, or **y** says /**j**/; **g** followed by **a** or **u** says /**g**/.

Teacher's Note: There are exceptions to this rule. Your student will learn more soft g words as he learns to read multi-syllable words.

h. Ask your student to fold a paper in half one way. Now, fold it in half the other way. Open the paper. Cut the paper as shown in the diagram.

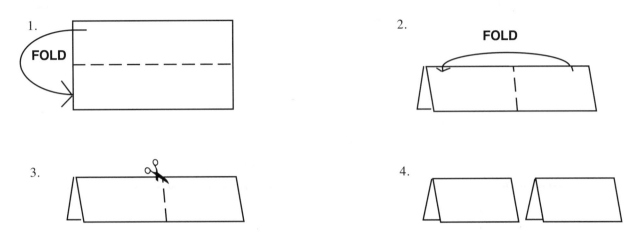

Ask your student to think about Max and Casey. Think about how they may have looked. On the front of one paper, your student may draw a simple picture of Max or write his name. On the front of the other paper, he will do the same with Casey. Give assistance as needed.

Now, on the inside of Max's picture, describe Max with some describing words. **Possible suggestions: peaceful, content, quiet, etc.**

On the inside of Casey's picture, describe Casey with some describing words. **Possible suggestions: fearful, loud, proud, etc.**

Day 5

a. Ask your student to tell you the story of "The Country Mouse's Big Adventure" in his own words. He may use the Story Folder, if needed.

b. Ask your student to think about a time when he visited a new place. It may have been good, but it may have been bad. Discuss this with your student. Then ask him to write or dictate to you, a few sentences telling about the visit.

c. Remind your student that nouns are naming words. They name a person, place, or thing. Using the sentences he wrote or dictated, ask him to underline all the nouns.

d. Remind your student that the name of a particular person, place, or thing is called a proper noun. Ask your student if he remembers how you begin a proper noun. **capital letter** Using the sentences he wrote or dictated, ask him to circle all the proper nouns.

e. Ask your student to look at these words as you read them aloud. Ask him to clap his hands for each syllable he hears and write down the number of syllables in each word:

1) *surprise* - **2**   2) *fishing* - **2**   3) *wonderful* - **3**
4) *orange* - **2**   5) *ducks* - **1**   6) *calendar* - **3**
7) *swim* - **1**   8) *table* - **2**

f. Ask your student to complete the puzzle by circling the hard **c** and **g** words in red and the soft **c** and **g** words in blue. Review the hard and soft sounds of **c** and **g**, if needed.
Possible words: Red - gas go goat got cut cute cat coat   Blue - gem gel gent cent city

g. Ask your student to choose "David and Goliath" or "The Country Mouse's Big Adventure" to act out. Make this as simple or elaborate as you and your student wish.

h. Ask your student to read the list of words: *red yellow apple blue*.

All the words belong together except one word. Ask your student to find the word that does not belong in the group, circle the word and tell why it did not belong. **apple - All the words are color words except *apple*. *Apple* is not a color; it does not belong.**

Once your student understands the directions, ask him to circle the word in each list that does not belong.

1) dog rose pig cat   **rose - It is not an animal.**
2) plate cup fork hot dog   **hot dog - It is not something we use to eat or drink.**
3) pencil hat pen marker   **hat - It is not a writing utensil.**
4) book socks shorts shirt   **book - It is not something you wear.**

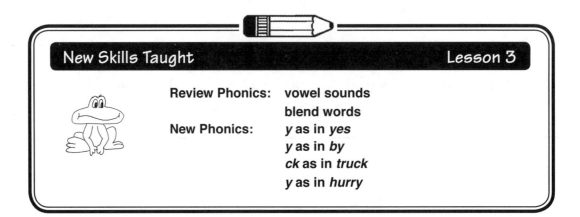

Review Phonics: vowel sounds
                  blend words
New Phonics: *y* as in *yes*
                  y as in *by*
                  ck as in *truck*
                  y as in *hurry*

Materials needed:
Little Bear by Else
Holmelund Minarik

craft materials

Day 1. b.
1) zoo
2) mother kangaroo and
   her baby
3) to rock it; to keep the
   baby safe

No, the pocket is a part
of the kangaroo's body.

Day 1

a. Read this poem to your student, or your student may read it
    to you.

> *Today when I*
> *Was at the zoo,*
> *I watched the Mother*
> *Kangaroo.*
>
> *Inside her skin*
> *She has a pocket.*
> *She puts her baby*
> *There, to rock it!*

"The Pocket" by Ilo Orleans from *The Zoo That Grew*
with permission of Karen S. Solomon

b. Talk with your student about the poem. You may use the
    following questions to help you in your discussion.

    1) *Where does the poem take place?*
    2) *What did the person see at the zoo?*
    3) *Why do you think Mother Kangaroo put the baby in her*
       pocket? Do you think her pocket is like the pocket you
       have on your clothes?

c. Review with your student that words that have the same
    sound, or syllable ending, are rhyming words. Read the
    first verse of the poem again to your student. Ask your
    student to underline the two words that rhyme. **zoo /**
    kangaroo

Now, read the second verse of the poem again to your student. Ask him to underline two words that rhyme in this verse. **pocket / it**

d. Read the following lines to your student. Ask your student to tell you a rhyming word to complete them.

1) *I see a mouse*
   He lives in my _____. **Possible answer: house**

2) *I see a cat*
   He sits on a _____. **Possible answers: mat or hat**

 Ask your student to illustrate the rhymes.

 e. Tell your student that he has learned two ways to spell words with the /**k**/ sound. Ask him if he remembers. **letter k, and letter c followed by a,o,u**

Tell your student that the letter combination **ck** can also make a /**k**/ sound. The **c** is a silent letter in this pair, so we only hear the /**k**/ sound. Say the words *pocket* and *rock*. Ask your student if he can hear the /**k**/ sound.

Find page 49 in the *Student Activity Book*. Ask your student to cut out the kangaroo and the pocket. Glue the pocket onto the kangaroo as directed.

Ask your student to fold a piece of paper in half lengthwise. Cut along the fold, so you have half a sheet. You may keep the other half for the next activity. Fold this half sheet in half widthwise. Fold it again widthwise. Fold it one more time widthwise. When you open the sheet, you should have seven folds. Cut along the folds. You should end up with eight strips of paper.

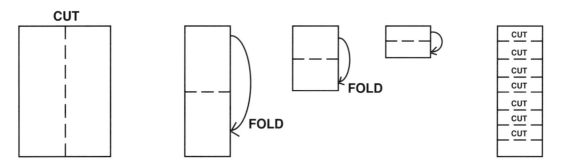

Ask your student to write the **ck** words listed below on the paper strips as you read the words. Read the words slowly. Give as much help as needed. Your student is learning to process the phonics he has learned and spell these new words: *rock neck sick sack duck sock deck pack.*

Upon completion and making any needed corrections, ask your student to place the word strips in the kangaroo's pocket. You will need the kangaroo again for **2e**.

f. Use this time to teach your student the basic steps to find information on a topic. If you have an encyclopedia, help your student look up the word *kangaroo*. Tell your student when looking up information in the encyclopedia, we look in the letter volume with which the word begins.

For example, when looking up information on dogs, we would look in the D volume. For cats, we would look in the C volume. Ask your student which volume he would need to use to find information on *kangaroos*. **K volume** Point out the guide words at the top of the page to help find the word.

Read the section on kangaroos to your student. After reading about kangaroos, ask your student to make a list, orally or in writing, of three facts, or true statements, about kangaroos.

Day 2

2. a. Read the poem to or with your student.

Mice

I think mice
Are rather nice.

Their tails are long,
Their faces small,
They haven't any
Chins at all.
Their ears are pink,
Their teeth are white,
They run about
The house at night
They nibble things
They shouldn't touch
And no one seems
To like them much.

But I think mice
Are nice.

by Rose Fyleman

b. Talk with your student about the poem. You may use the following questions to help you in your discussion.

1) *Why do you think this person likes mice?*
2) *Do you like mice? Why or why not?*

c. Ask your student if he remembers what a naming word is called. **noun** Tell your student that this poem has a lot of words which describe nouns. Ask him what word describes the mice's tails. Underline the word in red. **long** What word describes their faces? Underline the word in blue. **small** What word describes their ears? Underline the word in green. **pink** What word describes their teeth? Underline the word in yellow. **white**

d. Give your student the half sheet of paper from **1e**, or start again by following the same directions. See page 23 of this book.

Your student should begin with eight paper strips. Tell your student you are now going to dictate more **ck** words. These **ck** words contain blends. Again, help your student as needed: *brick truck speck smack stick shock pluck check.*

Upon completion and making any needed corrections, ask your student to place the paper strips in the kangaroo's pocket.

e. Tell your student that the letter **y** can make three different sounds. Read the words to or with your student: *yes fly funny.*

Teacher's Note: Your student may need help with the word *funny*.

Ask your student if he can tell you the three sounds of **y**. /y/, /ī/, and /ē/

The letter **y** can be pronounced as a consonant in the beginning of a word like *yes*. The letter **y** can also function as a vowel when it comes at the end of a word. It can say /ī/ as in *fly*; or it can say /ē/ as in *funny*.

Tell your student that in the poem, "Mice," there is a word that ends in **y**. Underline this word. **any** Ask your student to tell you the sound **y** makes in the word *any*. **long e sound**

f. Find page 53 in the *Student Activity Book*. Ask your student to cut out all the word cards for **2f**. Place the *long e, long i,* and **y** *like yard* cards side by side, making three columns. Read the words to your student, or he may read them to you. Circle the **y** in each word. Ask your student to put the cards in the correct column.

long e - only happy bunny jumpy sunny
long i - fly try by my spy
y like yard - yellow yak yell yo-yo yack yes

g. Tell your student that a fact is something that can be proven to be true. An opinion is what someone thinks or feels about something. Find page 51 in the *Student Activity Book*. Under the *Fact* column, ask your student to write or dictate true things about mice. He does not need to use complete sentences. Under the *Opinion* column, ask your student to write or dictate his own opinion about mice.

Ex:

Fact	**Opinion**
small	cutest little animal
runs fast	funny looking
little tail	scare me
quiet	etc.
etc.	

h. Your student may also take a survey. Explain that a survey is a process of asking people questions and recording them. Tell your student to ask as many people as he can, "Do you like mice?" Make two columns. Write *Like* and *Dislike* on the top of each column. Tell him to record the person's name and indicate if the person is a child or grown-up.

Ex:

Like	**Dislike**
Ted - child	Teacher - grown-up
Sam - child	Dan - child
Jill - child	

When he is finished with the survey, discuss it with him and look for any pattern he may have discovered.

Day 3

3. a. Read the poem to or with your student.

> *Little drops of water,*
> *Little grains of sand,*
> *Make the mighty ocean*
> *And the pleasant land.*

Mother Goose Rhyme

b. Find page 53 in the *Student Activity Book*. Ask your student to cut out the word cards for **3b**. You and your student can create additional cards using blank paper.

Make two columns on a sheet of paper. On the top of one column, write *Short Vowel Sound*; on the other column write *Long Vowel Sound*. Tell your student to put each word card in the correct column. If necessary, your student may use the picture cards from Lesson 1 to help identify the sounds.

Long Vowel Sound -   tube mole joke time wait mule game mice
Short Vowel Sound -   block spell smack glad spot trim brick glum
smell plug

c. Read the review sight words to your student: *your   another   have   what*.

The following sentences contain the review sight words. Ask your student to read them to you.

1) I need *another* ten cents.   2) *What* do you need?
3) I *have* a hole in my sock.   4) May I use *your* sock?

d. Remind your student that **k** and **ck** make a /**k**/ sound. Find the Kangaroo Pocket Activity from **1e**. Ask your student to read the **ck** words aloud.

e. Ask your student to read the words in the Phonics Word Box:
king sink dunk bank leak bike elk keg kiss.

f. Find page 55 in the *Student Activity Book*. Ask your student to cut out the word cards. Make two columns on a sheet of paper. At the top of one column write *s sounds like /s/*. On the top of the other column, write *s sounds like /z/*. Ask your student to place each word card in the correct column according to what sound the letter **s** makes. Upon completion, ask him to read the columns of words to you. Store in an envelope.
s sounds like /s/ - spot sat pass sweater
s sounds like /z/ - rose his was present

g. Give your student four pieces of paper. On the bottom of each paper, ask him to copy a line of the poem in **3a**. Ask him to use the space above his lines to draw a picture describing each line of poetry. Or he may use magazine clippings. When all the pages are done, tell him to stack the pages in order, and staple it along the edge.

Day 4

a. Read the story, "What Will Little Bear Wear?," from the book, *Little Bear,* to your student, or your student may read to you.

b. Talk with your student about the story. You may use the following questions to help you in your discussion.

　　1) *What clothes did Little Bear first put on?* **hat, coat, snow pants**
　　2) *What do you put on when you are cold?*

c. Ask your student if he remembers what kind of letter begins every sentence. **capital letter** Tell him that every sentence must end with a period if it is a telling sentence. Every sentence must end with a question mark if it is an asking sentence. A sentence may end with an exclamation mark to show strong feeling.

Ask your student to read these sentences. Ask him to rewrite the sentences, capitalizing the first word and ending with a period, question mark, or exclamation mark.

　　1) the man was hot　　　　**The man was hot.**
　　2) what shall I do　　　　**What shall I do?**
　　3) i want to swim　　　　**I want to swim! or .**

d. Tell your student that *cold* and *hot* are words of opposite meaning. They are called antonyms. Say each of the following words and ask your student to say a word of opposite meaning, or an antonym.

yes - **no**　　　　　　　*boy* - **girl**
night - **day**　　　　　*dirty* - **clean**
happy - **sad, unhappy**　　*early* - **late**
wet - **dry**

e. Context Words

Your student will begin to learn a few ways to read an unfamiliar word. These four clues are helpful:

　　1) What is the text about? What did the prior sentences talk about?
　　2) What are the beginning sounds and ending sounds?
　　3) What is the size of the word?
　　4) Are there any pictures to give a hint?

With these four helpful clues, your student will often be able to decode the word.

Read these sentences as your student looks with you. Move your finger along the words as you read. Stop before the italicized word. Wait to see if he can decode the unfamiliar word. If he does not get it immediately, try the four clues.

This is a beginning lesson, so do not pressure your student. Tell him the word if he does not know.

My uncle can tell me about space. He is an *astronaut*.

Ron fell off a tree. He was hurt. He had to go to the *hospital*.

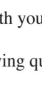

If you eat too much candy, you might get a *cavity*.

Day 5

a. Read the second story in *Little Bear*, "Birthday Soup," to or with your student.

b. Talk with your student about the story. You may use the following questions to help you in your discussion.

   1) *Who came to Little Bear's birthday party?*   **hen, duck, cat, and, of course, Mother Bear**
   2) Let your student look at the pictures to answer these questions: *Hen brought Little Bear some honey. What did Duck bring Little Bear?*   **a flower**
   3) *What did Cat bring Little Bear?*   **an apple**
   4) *How old is Little Bear?*   **six**

c. Find page 59 in the *Student Activity Book*. Ask your student to cut out the word cards for **5c** and glue them along the left-hand side of a sheet of paper.

Remind your student that a naming word is called a noun and that we add an **s** to the end of a word to mean more than one. This is called a plural noun. Ask him to read the first word, copy it next to the word card and make it plural, or mean more than one of that thing.

Ex: hat   hats
      girl   **girls**
      cup   **cups**
      hen   **hens**
      door   **doors**
      moon   **moons**
      stick   **sticks**
      boat   **boats**
      boy   **boys**

d. Find page 58 in the *Student Activity Book*. Ask your student to look at the picture and tell you what he sees in it. Ask him what he thinks happened just before this picture and what will happen just after it. Ask him to cut out the sentence strips on page 59 for **5d** and read the sentences. Then ask him to put the sentences in the order which would best explain the picture.

1) First, the ball went in the road.
2) Tim ran to the ball.
3) Tammy said, "Tim, stop!"
4) Tim was safe.

Your student may color the picture and glue the sentence strips under it.

e. Read the review sight words to your student: *does   down   put   ready*.

The following sentences contain the review sight words. Ask your student to read them to you.

1) *Does* the clock tick?   2) It fell *down* the stairs.
3) I will get *ready* to fix it.   4) No, *put* the clock in the trash.

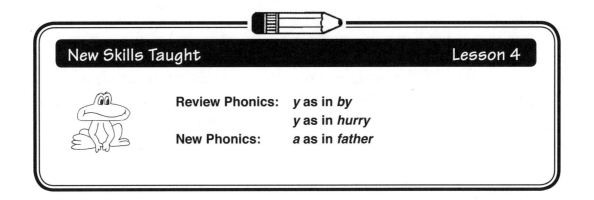

Review Phonics: *y* as in *by*

                      y as in *hurry*

New Phonics: *a* as in *father*

Day 1

a. Read the poem to or with your student.

> *Thirty days has September*
> *April, June, and November;*
> *All the rest have thirty-one.*
> *Except February alone,*
> *And that has twenty-eight days clear*
> *And twenty-nine in each leap year.*

Mother Goose Rhyme

b. Ask your student if he has heard this poem before. This poem helps us remember how many days are in each month. Ask your student to look at the poem, and show him names of the months. Ask him to underline them. Ask him if he notices anything special about them. **Months of the year begin with a capital letter.**

Tell your student that the names of the months begin with a capital letter because they name a particular month. They are proper nouns.

c. Show your student the number words in the poem. Ask him to circle them. Ask him if he notices anything different about the numbers *thirty-one*, *twenty-eight*, and *twenty-nine*. **They have hyphens.** Tell your student that number words from *twenty-one* to *ninety-nine* are written with hyphens.

d. Find page 61 in the *Student Activity Book*. Ask your student to cut out all the number cards and number word cards. Ask him to match the number card and the matching number word card, connecting the two number words. Glue them on a separate piece of paper and write the hyphens.

Materials Needed:
   Little Bear by Else Holmelund Minarik

✎ **Teacher's Note:** At the end of this lesson is Assessment 1. This covers all the Language Arts Skills covered in the first four lessons. Please evaluate your student's progress in phonics with the activities in the lesson. If he needs more review in phonics, take some time in the next two weeks to review the phonics needed.

e. Look at a calendar with your student or look on page 62 of the *Student Activity Book*. Show your student the name of each month. Say the month, and ask your student to repeat after you. Do the same with the days of the week. Tell your student that the name of months and days are proper nouns.

Ask your student to find his birthday month on the calendar, the current month, and the month of his favorite holiday, and write these months in the correct blank.

My birthday is in the month of _____. My favorite holiday is in the month of _____. Today is in the month of_____.

Ask your student to find out the birthdays of three people. Ask him to make a list of their names and their birthday months. Ask him to find their birthdays on the calendar. Help your student as needed.

f. Ask your student to look at this sentence as you read it to him.

1) *Birds fly*.

Ask your student to underline the doing word in the sentence. **fly**

Ask your student to look at these sentences as you read them aloud to him. After each sentence, ask him to underline the doing word.

2) *Rabbits* <u>**hop**</u>. 3) *Dogs* <u>**run**</u>. 4) *Children* <u>**play**</u>.

g. Ask your student if he remembers the three sounds the letter **y** can make. **y in** *yes***, long i as in** *fly***, and long e as in** *funny.*

Read the words aloud to your student:
twenty thirty forty fifty sixty seventy eighty ninety.

Ask your student what sound the letter **y** makes in these words. **y makes the long e sound**

h. **Art Adventure**
Ask your student to make a birthday card for someone who is having a birthday soon. Decorate with things you know the person likes. Help your student with any spelling for the inside of the card. Keep in a safe place, and when the birthday arrives, give it to the special person and say "Happy Birthday."

Day 2

a. Read the poem to your student, or your student may read it to you.

Written in March

The cock is crowing,
The stream is flowing,
The small birds twitter,
The lake doth glittter,
The green field sleeps in the sun;
The oldest and youngest
Are at work with the strongest;
The cattle are grazing,
Their heads never raising;
There are forty feeding like one!

William Wordsworth

b. Tell your student that we can add the letters **-ing** to the end of a doing word to show that something is still happening. Ask your student to find the words in the poem that end in **-ing** and circle them. **crowing, flowing, grazing, raising, feeding**

c. Ask your student to copy the words, adding the letters **-ing** to the end of each word.

1) read **reading** 2) paint **painting** 3) clean **cleaning** 4) sing **singing** 5) melt **melting**

 d. Your student has learned that the letter **a** can make two different sounds: ă as in *rag* and ā as in *bake*. Read these words to your student and ask him to tell you the **a** sound he hears in each one: rag **short a sound** bake **long a sound** The letter **a** can also make a third sound: ä as in *father*.

e. Read the review sight words to your student: *brown   love   zoo*.

The following sentences contain review sight words. Ask your student to read the sentences to you.

1) The man at the *zoo* will wash the cage.
2) I *love* to play with my father.
3) A yellow and *brown* wasp sat on my nose.

 f. Your student may choose "Written in March," "Thank You" (from Day 3), or any other poem to memorize. He may begin by copying the poem. He will work on his memorization tomorrow.

Day 3

a. Read the poem to or with your student.

Thank You

Thank you for the world so sweet,
Thank you for the food we eat,
Thank you for the birds that sing,
Thank you, God, for everything.

Mrs. E. Rutter Leathan

b. Tell your student that sometimes two words are joined together to make a new word. This is called a compound word. Read the poem again to your student, and move your finger along the words as you read it. Ask your student if he can find the compound word. Circle it. **everything**

c. Find page 67 in the *Student Activity Book*. Ask your student cut out the word cards for **3c** and read each one. Ask him to combine two of the cards to make a compound word. Do the same with the remaining words. He may glue them on a piece of paper and illustrate one of them. **mailman, baseball, homerun, cupcake**

d. When you add the letters **-ing** to the end of a word that ends with a silent **e**, you must first drop the **e** and then add **-ing**. Ex: share - sharing

Find page 67 in the *Student Activity Book*. Ask your student to cut out all the word cards and **-ing** cards for **3d**. Tell your student to lay the word cards in a vertical row and place the **-ing** cards over the word, covering the silent **e**, so that the spelling of the word will be correct. Do this for all the words.

Read the base word to your student, and ask your student to read the new word with the **-ing** ending. Tell him that the **-ing** ending tells us the action is happening now.

wave **waving**, smile **smiling**, live **living**, share **sharing**, taste **tasting**, bake **baking**

Teacher's Note: The base word is the main word without the suffix.

After you have completed the exercise together, ask your student to glue the word cards on a sheet of paper on the left-hand margin and glue the **-ing** endings in the correct place.

Upon completion, ask your student to read the new words and use each one in sentences. He may do this orally or in writing.

e. Context words

Tell your student that he will continue to learn to read unfamiliar words using the context clues:

1) What is the text about? What did the prior sentences talk about?
2) What are the beginning and ending sounds?
3) What is the size of the word?
4) Are there any pictures to give a hint?

Read these sentences to your student, moving your fingers along the words as you read. Stop when you get to the italicized word, and ask your student if he can tell you the word. Remind him to use the context clues, if needed.

1) The rain fell and fell. I was not wet. I had an *umbrella*.
2) I will dig a hole. I need a *shovel*.

 f. Ask your student to continue memorizing the poem.

Day 4

a. Read the story, "Little Bear Goes to the Moon," from the book, *Little Bear*.

b. Talk with your student about the story. You may use the following questions to help you in your discussion.

   1) *Did Little Bear really go to the moon?* **No, he imagined it.**
   2) *Little Bear pretended to fly to the moon. Do you ever pretend? Tell me about it.* **Answers will vary.**

c. Read the review sight words to your student: *which   white   you*.

The following sentences contain the review sight words. Ask your student to read them to you.

   1) *Which* way shall I go?
   2) Do you like the *white* cupcake?
   3) Will *you* come with me?

d. Find page 69 in the *Student Activity Book*. Your student will begin making his own calendar for this month. He may begin today and finish it tomorrow. You may photocopy this page for your student and make more months.

Teacher's Note: You may wish to choose the next month instead.

e. Ask your student to draw a picture that illustrates the poem he is memorizing.

Day 5

a. Read the story, "Little Bear's Wish," from the book, *Little Bear.*

b. Talk with your student about the story or any of the stories in *Little Bear.* You may use the following questions to help you in your discussion.

 1) *We have finished the book. How did Mother Bear show love for Little Bear?*
 2) *Which story was your favorite? Why?*

c. Ask your student to look at these sentences as you read them aloud. After you read a sentence, ask your student to tell you the doing word and underline it.

 1) *Little Bear **plays** in the snow.* 2) *Little Bear **makes** Birthday Soup.*
 3) *Little Bear **ate** his lunch.*   4) *Little Bear **sleeps**.*

  d. Today is poetry presentation day. Allow your student to display his illustration as he recites his poem.

e. Today, complete *Assessment 1* with your student.

Assessment 1
(Lessons 1 - 4)

1. *A noun is a person, place, or thing. I will read three words to you. Tell me which word is a noun: yellow happy dog.* **dog**

2. *A proper noun names a particular person, place, or thing. The word* boy *is a person. Tell me a name of a particular person.* **Answers will vary.**

3. *How do you begin a person's name?* **a capital letter**

4. *An antonym is a word of opposite meaning. Tell me an antonym for these words: short* **tall**; *float* **sink**; *loud* **quiet**; *wet* **dry**. *(These are only possible answers.)*

5. *A compound word is two words joined together to make a new word. What are the two words in these compound words: doghouse* **dog and house,** *mousetrap* **mouse and trap,** *rainbow* **rain and bow**.

6. *Tell me two words to describe a cat.* **Possible answers: white, black, fat, little, cute.**

7. *Repeat these words after me. Clap your hands for each syllable you hear. How many syllables are in these words: hamburger -* **3**, *carrot -* **2**, *joke -* **1**

8. *Tell me a rhyming word for these words: lake -* **rake, make sake, wake, etc**; *went -* **bent, sent, lent, dent, etc.**, *man -* **can, ban, fan, pan, etc**.

9. *A pronoun is a word that takes place of a noun. Listen to this sentence: Mary swam in the pool. Now, tell me the sentence again, replacing Mary with a pronoun. Repeat the sentence as necessary.* **She swam in the pool**.

10. *Which letter volume of encyclopedia would you use to find information on these topics: rabbits -* **R volume**, *Texas -* **T volume**, *hurricanes -* **H volume**.

11. *A fact is a statement that is true. An opinion is a personal feeling about something. Tell me one fact about yourself. Tell me an opinion about yourself.* **Answers will vary**.

12. *What type of letter begins every sentence?* **a capital letter**

13. *Every sentence ends with a period, question mark, or exclamation mark. I will read three sentences. Tell me what punctuation mark goes at the end of each sentence.*

   You are a kind person. **a period**
   When is your birthday? **a question mark**
   Wow, let's have a party! **an exclamation mark**

14. *A plural noun is a naming word that means more than one. If I have more than one apple, I have many apples. The letter* **s** *is added to the end of the word. If you have more than one cat, what do you have?* **cats**

15. *How do you begin the months of the year, like January, February, etc.?* **a capital letter**
   How do you begin the days of the week, like Sunday, Monday, etc.? **a capital letter**

Introduction to Part 2

In the next 21 lessons, your student will be using four books from the *Successful Reading Series* to learn phonics, grammar, writing, and thinking skills. Use the phonics instruction as it is needed by your student. The review and new phonics skills are listed in each lesson for your convenience.

As in Part 1, you are asked to read the stories, passages, or activities to or with your student. This material was carefully chosen. Your student will benefit from the lesson activity whether he is a fluent or beginning reader. If he begins to read aloud and has difficulty with a word, simply tell him the word at that time. If you insist that he sound out the word, he will lose the flow of the reading. Make a note that he needs instruction on the sounds in that word and work on it later. When your student reads aloud, it is best to make it a successful and enjoyable experience.

On Day 5, your student is asked to read the story aloud. If your student is not a fluent reader, please read every other page aloud to him. He will grow in his reading skills as he follows along with you, and he will read enough so you can evaluate how well he is learning new skills. Celebrate his success by adding to his Reading Chart. To do this, pull out page 375 of the *Student Activity Book*, write your student's name on the top, mount it on construction paper and post it on a wall. When your student reads a story aloud, ask him to color the corresponding picture on the Reading Chart. When all the story pictures are colored, glue the correct Reader Cover on his Reading Chart. The Reader Covers are found on the back cover of the *Student Activity Book*.

If your student is a fluent reader, or reading above grade level, ask him to read the story aloud on Day 1 of all the language arts lessons. Throughout the week, use only the phonics instruction that he needs. Then on Day 5, you can skip the reading aloud of the reader and go on with the rest of the lesson. Encourage your student to read as many books as he can at this level. Even if this level is below his reading level, this is an important step in your student's reading education. This Fluency Stage is a time to cement the skills learned and is vital preparation for further success in reading. Allow your student to read as many "easy books" as he can and be confident that the Fluency Stage of reading will pay off richly in the future.

Included in most of the lessons are *Enrichment Activities* to expand your student's thinking, reasoning, and writing skills. These activities are excellent for the fluent student who is not completing the phonics lessons. They will be beneficial for the beginning reader as well. Ask him to dictate his thoughts to you as you write these thoughts. Please use these activities as you desire.

Handwriting is introduced in Part 2, with a review of all letters and numbers. A sentence and matching picture handwriting sheet is included in every week's lesson. Your student can use his best handwriting to proudly display his work. Please do not insist on the very best handwriting all the time from your student. He is concentrating on learning many new skills.

Weekly spelling words are included in each lesson. Activities and puzzles review the words with your student each day. You may give a traditional spelling test each Friday if a spelling grade is needed. Otherwise, we suggest you evaluate your student's ability using the puzzles and activities.

Successful Reading Series used in Part 2

All Around the Farm
Forest Fables
In, Out, and About Catfish Pond
Up, Down, and Around the Rain Tree

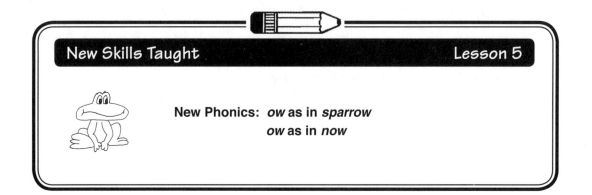

New Skills Taught   **Lesson 5**

New Phonics: *ow* as in *sparrow*
ow as in *now*

Day 1

1. a. Find the story, "Will Little Sparrow Fly?" from the reader *All Around the Farm.* Read it to or with your student.

   b. Talk to your student about the story. You may use these questions to help you in your discussion.

      1) *Tell me this story in your own words.* Allow your student to use the pictures if needed.
      2) *What is Little Sparrow trying to do?* **fly**
      3) *Even though Mama said he would fly one day, he has doubts. Why does he doubt?* **Brown Chick tells him he can't fly.**
      4) *How does Pig help Little Sparrow overcome his doubts?* **Pig told him a story about Little Sparrow's past. Pig told him that Little Sparrow had learned to do new things and how truthful Mama had been in the past.**
      5) *Why did Little Sparrow have to wait before he could fly?* **He had to grow bigger and stronger before he was ready to fly.**
      6) *Why did he still try everyday?* **He didn't know when he would be ready to fly, so he tried everyday.**
      7) *Was Little Sparrow a failure when he tried everyday and still fell down? Why or why not?*
      8) *Did you like the story? Was there anything you didn't like about it? Explain it to me.*
      9) *Can you tell me some things you can easily do now that you could not do two years ago, such as ride a bike, skate, read, write, etc.?*

   c. Ask your student, to write or dictate two to three sentences telling what he can do now that he could not do two years ago. Write them on blank paper so he can draw pictures on the paper.

Materials needed:
All Around the Farm

An optional activity involves using photos of your student at various ages.

d. Ask your student to look at this passage as you read it aloud.

> *Little Sparrow called to Pig, "How do you like this try?"*
> *"It is time for you to fly, Little Sparrow," smiled Pig.*

Ask your student to find the word in the first sentence that tells what Little Sparrow did and circle it. **called**

The letters **-ed** have been added to the end of the word *call* to mean something has already been done. The **-ed** makes the sound /**d**/ in *called*.

Ask your student to find the word in the second sentence that tells what Pig did as he yelled to Little Sparrow and circle it. **smiled**

The word *smiled* is spelled *s-m-i-l-e* without **ed** added to the end of the word. Can you think of a rule for adding **-ed** to the word *smile*? If a word ends in a silent **e**, drop the **e** before adding **-ed**. The **-ed** makes the sound /**d**/ in *smiled*.

Ask your student to add **-ed** to these words, remembering the new rule he learned about the silent **e**: 1) *bake* **baked** 2) *dance* **danced** 3) *love* **loved** 4) *race* **raced** 5) *wave* **waved** 6) *hope* **hoped** Say the new words, and then act them out.

e. Ask your student to copy the spelling words for this week. Read them to or with your student: *kit call keg cut.*

Day 2

2. a. Review the story "Will Little Sparrow Fly?" with your student.

b. Find the pictures for **2b** on page 77 in the *Student Activity Book*. Ask your student to cut them out. Talk to your student about each picture, asking him what he sees in the picture and what is happening. Ask your student, to put the pictures in the order in which they happened. He may use the reader, if needed.

c. In the story, Pig tells Little Sparrow, "Come here, Little Sparrow, I have a tale to tell you." The word *tale* means a story, like a fairy tale. Can you think of a word that sounds the same as *tale* but has a different meaning? **tail**

Ask your student what this *tail* means. Both words have a long /$\bar{a}$/ sound, but they are spelled differently and have different meanings. Words that sound the same but have different meanings are called **homonyms**.

Teacher's Note: Some grammar books refer to these words as homophones.

Tell your student that since we can't tell any difference by listening to these kind of words, we have to find other ways to know the meaning of the word. One way is to look up the word in the dictionary. Usually, we can understand the meaning of a word by looking at how the word is used in the sentence. By using the clues in the sentence, we often know the meaning of the word.

Read the following sentence to your student and ask him which word is used in this sentence: tail or tale. The bird has a long tail. **t-a-i-l**

d. Ask your student to read these words and tell what he thinks they mean: *meet meat one won*

e. How Do You Spell That Word?

Give your student a piece of paper and a pencil. You will dictate the spelling words to him, guiding him through the process of spelling the words. Read any of the following sections your student needs.

*We know that the letters **c** and **k** can make the /k/ sound at the beginning of a word. So how do you know when to use a **c** and when to use a **k**? If the letter after the /k/ sound is an **e** or **i**, the /k/ sound is usually spelled with the letter **k**. If the /k/ sound is followed by **a**, **o** or **u** use the letter **c**. Let's try these words.*

1) *cut - This word begins with a /k/ sound. What vowel sound do you hear after the /k/? If the /k/ sound is followed by an **e** or **i**, the word begins with a **k**; otherwise it begins with the letter **c**.* If your student has difficulty with the word, repeat the rule.
2) *keg -* If needed, repeat the rule given in 1.
3) *kit -* If needed, repeat the rule given in 1.
4) *call -* If needed, repeat the rule given in 1.

f. Look at the title of the story again. The word *Sparrow* ends with an /ō/ sound. Ask your student how he thinks the /ō/ sound is spelled in *Sparrow*. **ow**

The letters **ow** make two different sounds. The **ow** can say /ō/ as in *Sparrow* or /ow/ as in *now*. Ask your student to read the words in the Phonics Word Box. Tell him to try the /ō/ sound and the /ow/ sound to decide which one is correct: *cow now low blow plow own   how down   grow*.

Teacher's Note: If he has difficulty, tell him the word. A word like *now* may be difficult.

g. If possible, have your student look at four or five photographs of himself taken at several different ages. Ask him to put the pictures in order from youngest to oldest and to tell you the differences he sees from picture to picture. If these photos can be used, glue them on paper in order from youngest to oldest.

Ask your student to write his age under each picture. This may be continued in a book or notebook form as a personal timeline.

h. Find page 75 in the *Student Activity Book*. Ask your student to complete the page by tracing the letters and writing them twice on the same line. Trace the words and write them once.

Day 3

a. Review the story "Will Little Sparrow Fly?" with your student. Ask your student to look at the map in the front of the reader.

1) *Can you find the farmhouse? barn? sheep pasture?* **Refer to map.**
2) *If you walked out of the farmhouse door, how would you get to the chicken coop? the barn? the doghouse?* **Refer to map.**
3) *If you walked out of the barn and turned right, where would you be?* **Refer to map.**

b. Review the uses of the period, question mark, and exclamation mark. A period (.) goes at the end of a telling sentence. A question mark (**?**) goes at the end of an asking sentence. An exclamation mark (**!**) goes at the end of a sentence that tells something very exciting or important.

Find page 77 in the *Student Activity Book*. Ask your student to cut out the sentence strips and punctuation cards for **3b**. Glue the sentence cards on the left side of a piece of paper. These sentences have no ending punctuation mark. Read the sentences with your student and ask him to glue the correct punctuation card at the end of each sentence.

c. In this lesson there are three sight words that your student needs to learn: *would could should*. Read the words with your student.

Ask him to read the sentences to you. Review the sight words throughout the week if needed.

1) *Would* you like some cake?
2) *Could* he go with us?
3) *Should* I take my coat?

d. Ask your student to say the word *sparrow*. Ask him how many syllables he hears in the word. Tell him to clap for each syllable. **two syllables** Tell your student the following syllable rule.

Syllable Sense: If a word has two of the same consonants in the middle of the word, divide the word between them. Ask him to divide sparrow. **spar/row**

Ask your student to say the word *below*. Ask him how many syllables he hears in the word. **two syllables**

Syllable Sense: If the first syllable of a word ends with a vowel, the vowel will usually say its long sound. Ex: table **ta/ble**

When a syllable ends with a vowel, the vowel says its name. In the word *below* the letter **e** says its name.

Find page 77 in the *Student Activity Book* for **3d**. Using the two Syllable Sense rules, ask your student to draw a line where the word should be divided. After you check the line, ask him to cut the word apart and glue the pieces on blank paper. Read the list of words with your student. **ta/ble   lit/tle   spar/row   be/low   hid/den   be/hind**

e. Ask your student to draw a simple map of his room or yard, using the story map as an example. Ask him to write or dictate labels for the map.

f. Complete the Spelling Words Puzzle. Ask your student to fill in the blank with a spelling word that rhymes with the italicized word.

1) I have a little *bit*. I will put it in a **kit**.
2) I will play *ball* until I hear my mother **call**.
3) He lives in a *hut*. He uses an ax to **cut**.
4) Dad has a strong *leg* to kick the wooden **keg**.

g. Find page 76 in the *Student Activity Book*. Ask your student to trace the sentence at the top of the page.

Day 4

a. Review the Word List below for "Will Little Sparrow Fly?" with your student.

   how now down below sparrow who called smiled

b. Find the Story Folder, "Farley's Trick," in the *Student Activity Book,* page 79. Read the story to or with your student.

c. Talk to your student about the story, or you may use these questions to help you in your discussion.

   1) *Tell me the story using your own words.*
   2) *Is this story real or make-believe? How do you know?* **make-believe, the animals talk**
   3) *If you were Connie in the story, how would you feel at the end of the story?*
   4) *What do you think of Farley's trick? Do you think it was a good trick or not? Tell me why you think that.*
   5) *The man who first told this story lived a long time ago. He wrote it to teach a lesson. What do you think he wanted to teach in this story?* **Do not listen to flattery.**
   6) *How would you describe the fox?* **Possible answer: sly, sneaky, deceiving**
   7) *How would you describe the crow?* **Possible answer: proud, vain, not very smart**

d. Read the homonyms with your student. Review the meaning of each word. Ask your student to write or dictate a sentence about "Farley's Trick" using some of these words: *piece peace heard herd road rode*.

e. Help your student number a piece of paper 1 - 5. Dictate the spelling words to your student. If he has any difficulty at all, use the same process used in **2e**. This is not a test, just another way to help your student learn how to spell. *kit cat key call*

f. Find page 76 in the *Student Activity Book*. Ask your student to begin copying the sentence on the bottom line and coloring the picture. He can complete the page in one or two days.

Day 5

a. Ask your student to read "Will Little Sparrow Fly?" aloud. Celebrate his success and add to his Reading Chart.

b. Read these words to your student and ask him to divide them into syllables.
Ex: la / ter; lit / tle

1) din / ner 2) be / cause 3) yum / my 4) pre / tend 5) bel / ly 6) o / pen

c. Review "Farley's Trick," using the Story Folder if needed. Ask your student to tell you about each character in the story. Help him take his description and put it into one sentence. Ask him to write or dictate that sentence for each picture.

d. Using props, such as a chair for the tree, and paper for the cheese, help your student act out "Farley's Trick" with someone else.

e. Ask your student to look at the picture, read the sentences, and decide which sentence best describes the picture.

___ 1) The hills are far away.
___ 2) The branch is thin.
__X__ 3) How the sparrow can sing!
___ 4) The big tree is brown.

f. Optional: Spelling test

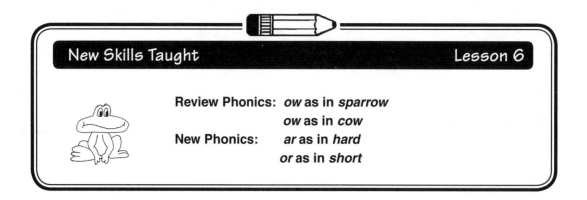

Review Phonics: *ow* as in *sparrow*
                     ow as in *cow*
New Phonics: *ar* as in *hard*
                     or as in *short*

Materials Needed:
All Around the Farm

Day 1

a. Find the story "Hard, Short Hay" from the reader, *All Around the Farm*. Read it to or with your student.

b. Talk to your student about the story, or you may use these questions to help you in your discussion.

1) *Tell me the story in your own words.* Allow him to use the pictures if needed. **Self-explanatory**
2) *How would you describe Son?* **Allow for discussion.**
3) *How would you describe Mama Cow?* **Allow for discussion.**
4) *What problem does Mama Cow have at the beginning of the story?* **Son will not make his hay bed.** *How does she solve the problem?* **She decides not to make the bed for him.**
5) *Do you think her way of solving the problem is a good idea? Why or why not?* **Answers will vary.**
6) *What did Son decide to do about his hay bed at the end of the story? Why?* **Son decided to make his bed because he could not sleep in an uncomfortable, hard, smelly bed.**

c. Ask your student to look at this sentence.

He was playing with a dog.

The letters **-ing** have been added to the end of the word *play* to mean that the action is going on now. For many words, we just add **-ing** to the end of the word.

Ex: sleep - sleeping

Ask your student to look to this sentence.

The short hay was poking him.

The word *poking* is spelled *poke* before adding **-ing**. Ask your student if he can think of a rule for adding **-ing** to the word *poke*. If there is a silent **e** at the end of a word, drop the **e** and then add **-ing**.
Ex: drive   driving

Ask your student to add **-ing** to the words listed, say the new word, and then act it out:

smile - **smiling**, jump - **jumping**, smell - **smelling**, vote - **voting**, call - **calling**.

d. Find page 81 of the *Student Activity Book*. Ask your student to read the words in the Phonics Word Box and use them to fill in the blanks in the sentences: *now   cow   blow   row*.

1) The **cow** ate hay.
2) The cats sat in a **row**.
3) We have to go **now**.
4) The wind did **blow**.

e. Find page 82 in the *Student Activity Book*. Ask your student to copy the spelling words for this week. Read them to or with your student: *row   blow   boat   poke*.

Day 2

a. Review the story, "Hard, Short Hay."

b. There are three main characters in the story. Discuss them with your student, using these questions.

1) *Which characters, or animals, in the story do you remember?* **Mama Cow, Son, Goat**
2) *What do you remember about each character?*
3) *Why didn't Son want to do his chore?* **He could not see the sense in making his bed every day.**
4) *How would you have felt if you were Son in this story? Would you want to spread out the bed and then make it again everyday? Why or why not?*

c. Find page 82 in the *Student Activity Book*. Ask your student to look at each picture and write or dictate a sentence about each character.

d. Read this sentence with your student.

Mama Cow couldn't see Son at all.

In this sentence, there is a word with an apostrophe (') in it. Ask your student to circle the word. **Couldn't** When we put two words together to make a shortened word, we use an apostrophe (') to show that we have left out letter(s). This new word is called a **contraction**.

Find page 87 in the *Student Activity Book*. On one side is a list of word combinations, and the other side has a list of contractions. Ask your student to cut out the word combinations and the contractions for **2d**. Ask him to match the word combinations to the contraction that they will make. Check his work. Ask him to glue the word cards on paper, side by side.

e. How Do You Spell That Word?

Give your student a piece of paper. Dictate the spelling words and read the following sections your student needs.

*There are several letter combinations that sound like /ō/: **oa**, **ow**, **o_e**. If the /ō/ sound is at the end of the word, it is usually spelled with **ow**. If the /ō/ sound is in the middle of the word, use **oa** or **o_e**. Let's try these words.*

1) *boat - Where do you hear the /ō/ sound? Is it at the end or in the middle of the word? Since it is in the middle, the /ō/ sound is probably spelled with **oa** or **o**, consonant, and silent **e**. Tell your student how to spell it if needed.*
2) *row - Where is the /ō/ sound? Since it is at the end, it is probably spelled with an **ow**.*
3) *blow - If needed, repeat the rule from 2.*
4) *poke - If needed, repeat the rule from 1.*

f. Look at the title of our story again: "Hard, Short Hay." The word *hard* has the letters **ar** in the middle of it. These letters say **/ar/** as in *car* most of the time. Ask your student to look through the story and find three more words with **ar** in them, and say each word. **barn, yard, smart, sharp**

g. The word *short* has the letters **or** in the middle of it. These letters say **/or/** as in *fort* most of the time. Ask your student to look through the story and find two more words with **or** in them, and say each word. **chore, for**

h. Find page 85 in the *Student Activity Book*. Ask your student to complete the page by tracing each letter and writing it twice on the same line. Trace each word and write it once.

Day 3

a. Review the story for this week.

b. Review how Son learned the importance of doing his chore. Ask your student if he has ever learned this way. Spend some time talking about your student's lesson and any you can remember from your life.

c. Ask your student to read the story title again. One of the words in the title is the name of a thing. Ask him if he can tell you that word. Underline the word. **hay** Ask him to look through the story and find five naming words, or nouns and copy them on page 83 of the *Student Activity Book*. **Possible answers: Mama, Cow, dog, Goat, gate, Son, stall, bed, hay, yard, barn, smile, sun, day**

d. Ask your student if Son made his bed everyday and Mama Cow made her bed everyday, how many beds were made by the Cow family? **two beds**

Tell your student that we usually add the letter **s** to a naming word, or noun, to show that we mean more than one.

Ask your student to make each of these words mean more than one by copying each word and adding the letter **s** to the end of the word: kit - **kits**, cow - **cows**, chore - **chores**.

e. Context Words: *son, off, why*. Read these sentences to your student, moving your fingers along the words as you read. Stop when you get to the italicized word, and ask your student if he can tell you the word. Remind him to use the context clues, if needed.

> 1) What is the text about? What did the prior sentences talk about?
> 2) What are the beginning and ending sounds?
> 3) What is the size of the word?
> 4) Are there any pictures to give you a hint?

1) Our family went to the beach. My daughter and *son* played in the sand.
2) I put on my raincoat when I left the house. Since it stopped raining, I will take it *off*.
3) I asked my teacher, "*Why* do we have to do this math?"

f. Complete the Spelling Words Puzzle. Using the Code Box ask your student to put the correct letter in each blank below to complete the sentences.

Code Box									
a	b	e	k	l	o	p	r	t	w
1	2	3	4	5	6	7	8	9	10

The wind will not <u>b</u> <u>l</u> <u>o</u> <u>w</u>, so we have to <u>r</u> <u>o</u> <u>w</u> the <u>b</u> <u>o</u> <u>a</u> <u>t</u>.
                   2 5 6 10   8 6 10   2 6 1 9

You will have to <u>p</u> <u>o</u> <u>k</u> <u>e</u> the oar in the water.
                       7 6 4 3

g. Find page 86 in the *Student Activity Book* and ask him to trace the sentence on the top of the page.

Day 4

a. Review the Word List below for "Hard, Short Hay."

chore for short yard hard smart Son off why playing poking

b. Find page 87 in the *Student Activity Book*. Read these sentences with your student.

> *Mama Cow spoke to Son in a nice way. "The hay is now hard and short. You will not sleep well in a bed of hard, short hay. It smells, too."*

Ask your student to find the two words in the passage above that sound the same but are spelled differently and circle them. **to, too** These words also mean something different. Use the dictionary to find out the meanings if your student doesn't know them. **to - in the direction of, too - also, besides**

Ask your student if he can think of another word that sounds like *to* and *too* but is spelled differently and has another meaning. **two** Ask your student to fill in the blanks with *to*, *too*, or *two*.

   1) We went **to** the store.
   2) I want to go, **too**.
   3) I will buy **two** pies.

c. Find page 91 in the *Student Activity Book*. Follow the directions to make the Corn Barn Word Wheel. Turn the wheel and read the words to or with your student.

   d. Ask your student to use the Corn Barn Word Wheel to make four words and list them. Ask him to write sentences about our story using these four words. He can trace pictures from the reader for the sentences.

e. Help your student number a piece of paper 1 - 4. Dictate the spelling words to your student. If he has any difficulty at all, use the same process used in **2e**. *poke blow boat row*

f. Find page 86 in the *Student Activity Book* and ask your student to copy the sentence on the bottom line and color the page. He may take two days to complete this assignment.

Day 5

a. Ask your student to read "Hard, Short Hay" aloud. Celebrate his success and add to his Reading Chart.

b. Find page 90 in the *Student Activity Book*. In this picture, you see a boy doing a chore. Talk to your student about the picture, or you may use the following questions to help you in your discussion.

1) *How does the boy feel?*
2) *Why is he cleaning the van?*
3) *What may have happened before the picture?*
4) *What may have happened after the picture?*

   c. Ask him to write or dictate two sentences about the picture. Ask your student to read the words listed: 1) eye 2) ear 3) leg 4) toe 5) arm 6) hand. Ask him to copy the word and add the letter **s** to the end of each word to mean more than one: *eye* - **eyes**, *ear* - **ears**, *leg* - **legs**, *toe* - **toes**, *arm* - **arms**, *hand* - **hands**.

   Ask him to draw a picture of himself, a friend, or a made-up person. Label, or write, the body part word, next to the body parts. Remember, he is using the body part names with an **s** on the end so he will have to draw a line from the word to both of the body parts.

d. Optional: Spelling test

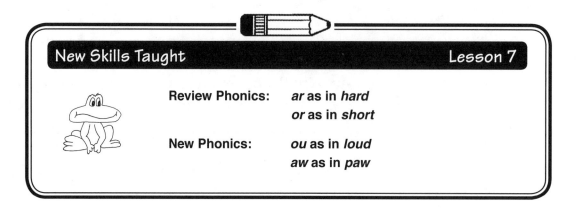

New Skills Taught   **Lesson 7**

Review Phonics:	*ar* as in *hard*
	or as in *short*
New Phonics:	*ou* as in *loud*
	aw as in *paw*

Materials Needed:
All Around the Farm

The Bravest Dog Ever
by Natalie Standiford

a globe, map, or atlas.

Day 1

a. Find the story, "Hound Dog Takes the Job," from the reader, *All Around the Farm*. Read it to or with your student.

b. Discuss the story with your student.

  1) *Tell me the story in your own words.* **Self-explanatory**
  2) *Why was Horse upset about Cat not doing her job?* **The mice were eating all the food.**
  3) *Why didn't Cat do her job? Why do you think she felt this way?* **She was daydreaming about the city. She thought it was a better life.**
  4) *When Hound Dog wanted the job, how did the other animals react?* **They laughed.** *Why?* **He didn't look like he could do the job.**
  5) *Why did Hound Dog smile at the end of the story?* **He and all the animals thought he did a good job.**
  6) *What do you think will happen to Cat now that she has no job?* **Answers will vary.**

c. Read this passage with your student.

  Cat opened one eye. With a yawn, she lifted a paw.

Two words end in **-ed**. Ask your student to circle both words. In the first word, *opened*, the **-ed** sounds like **/d/**. Say the word *lifted* and ask your student what sound **-ed** makes in that word. **/ed/** Tell him that sometimes when **-ed** is added to the end of a word it sounds like **/ed/**. Ask your student to copy the words in his *Student Activity Book* and add **-ed** to each one.

Then read them with or to your student:
shout - **shouted**, pour - **poured**, add - **added**, climb - **climbed**, turn - **turned**.

d. Read this passage with your student.

> *Mouse ran out of the house. He ran around the yard. He ran into the barn. He stopped when he found some straw and corn.*

There is one word with **-ed** at the end. Ask your student to circle it. The word is spelled s-t-o-p without the **-ed**. Ask your student if he knows why the letter **p** is doubled when we add the **-ed**. There is a rule that tells us a one-syllable word like *stop*, which ends with one short vowel and one consonant, must double its last consonant before adding **-ed** or **-ing**. In this word the **-ed** sounds like **/t/**.

Ask your student to copy each word and add **-ed** and **-ing** to the end of each word. Then read the words to or with your student:
hop - **hopped hopping**, mop - **mopped mopping**, rub - **rubbed rubbing**, rob - **robbed robbing**, rip - **ripped ripping**.

e. Find page 94 in the *Student Activity Book*. Ask your student to read the words in the Phonics Word Box and then fill in the blanks using one of the words: *corn barn more farm horse*.

   1) I wish I could ride a **horse**.
   2) I love pie. May I have some **more** of it?
   3) On a **farm**, the hay is kept in the **barn**.
   4) Dad loves **corn** on the cob.

f. Ask your student to copy the spelling words for this week. Read each one to or with him: *out how loud cow*.

Day 2

a. Review the story for this week with your student.

b. Find page 97 in the *Student Activity Book*. Ask your student to cut out the pictures and put them in the correct order on the table. Discuss each picture. Ask him to glue the pictures on paper, and write or dictate a sentence about each one.

c. Find page 97 in the *Student Activity Book*. Ask your student to cut out all the letter and word cards for **2c**. Put **/ed/**, **/d/**, and **/t/** next to each other. Read a word card to or with your student and ask him to place it below the correct sound which the **-ed** makes in the word.
/d/ - waved smiled loved /ed/ - painted landed dusted /t/ - baked hopped jumped

d. Read this passage with your student.

> *"The mice are eating all the straw and corn. The mice get fat, and I get thin," moaned Horse. He made a loud sound to arouse Cat.*

There are three words in this passage that use **ou** in the middle of the word. Ask your student to circle each one. **loud, sound, arouse**

The letters **ou** go together to make a different sound than **o** and **u** make by themselves. They say /**ow**/ as in *loud*. Say these words with your student: *hound   loud   sound   arouse   found   house.*

e. Read the first sentence of the passage in **2d** to or with your student. There is a word that ends in **aw** in the passage. Ask your student to circle it. **straw** The letters **aw** will often come at the end of a word and say /**aw**/ as in *paw*. Say these words with your student: *straw, paw, yawn, saw, jaw, claw.*

f. How Do You Spell That Word?

Give your student a piece of paper. You will dictate the spelling words to him guiding him through the process. Read the following sections that your student needs to correctly spell the words.

*There are two ways to spell the /**ow**/ sound: **ow** and **ou**. Both can be used in the beginning or middle of a word, but only **ow** is used at the end of a word.*

Teacher's Note: The exceptions are few, such as *thou*.

1) *how - Where do you hear the /**ow**/ sound? Since it is at the end of the word, it is spelled **ow**.*
2) *loud - Where do you hear the /**ow**/ sound? Since it is in the middle of the word, it may be spelled **ou**.*
3) *out - Where do you hear the /**ow**/ sound? Since it is in the beginning, it may be spelled **ou**.*
4) *cow - Use the rule in 1 as needed.*

g. Find page 99 in the *Student Activity Book* and ask your student to complete it.

Day 3

a. Review the story for this week.

b. Discuss Hound Dog with your student.

   1) *What do the animals think of Hound Dog in the beginning of the story?* **They don't think he can do the job.** *How do you know?* **They laugh at the idea.**
   2) *How does Pig react?* **Pig wants to give him a chance.**
   3) *Why do you think Pig wants to give Hound Dog a chance?* **He is wise and sees that Hound Dog wants to do the job.**
   4) *How does Hound Dog prove himself as a worker? Does he believe the other animals or himself?* **He works very hard and does not let their opinions get him down.**
   5) *What do the other animals think of Hound Dog at the end of the story?* **They think he is a good worker.**

c. Discuss with your student what Hound Dog was like at the beginning of the story and what he was like at the end. How had he changed and why did he make that change?

   Ask him to look at the pictures and write a sentence about Hound Dog telling how he felt in the beginning of the story. Below the other picture, write another sentence about how he felt at the end of the story.

d. Context Words: *some, eye, animals*. Read the words with your student. Ask him to read the sentences. Remind him to use the context clues as needed.

   1) I have ten cupcakes. Do you want *some*?
   2) We went to the zoo. We saw some *animals*.
   3) The branch fell down. I got some bark in my *eye*.

e. Syllable Sense

   Remind your student that if the first syllable of a word ends with a vowel, the vowel will usually say its long sound. Ex: e / ven.

   Usually the first vowel says its name, but not always. Ask your student to listen to each word as you read it and tell you how many syllables it has: *away open below belong*. **All the words have two syllables**.

   Ask your student to draw a line between the letters where the word is divided. Then ask him to say each word. **1) a / way   2) o / pen   3) be / low   4) be / long Teacher's Note: Some students may say *away* with a short *a* sound. This is acceptable.**

f. Read this passage with your student.

> *When he saw a mouse, he chased it far away from the barn. Hound Dog's loud growl made the mice afraid to come back.*
> *All week, Hound Dog kept the mice away. One day, he could hear the barn animals speaking. "He is a fine dog," said Cow.*
> *"What a dog!" said Hen.*
> *"He is the best dog," said Goat.*
> *Hound Dog smiled from ear to ear. He was proud to be a hound dog.*

Ask your student to circle the word that tells what kind of growl made the mice afraid. **loud** Circle the word that describes what kind of dog Cow called Hound Dog. **fine** Circle the word that describes what kind of dog Goat called Hound Dog. **best**. The last line has a word that describes Hound Dog. Circle that word. **proud**.

g. A word that describes something is called an adjective. Adjectives tell what kind, which one, or how many. Look around the room and find five things that you can better tell about by using a describing word, or an adjective.
Ex: clean desk, red book, happy child

h. Ask your student to complete the Spelling Words Puzzle.

1) out   2) cow   3) how   4) loud

i. Find page 100 in the *Student Activity Book* and have your student trace the sentence on the top of the page.

Day 4

a. Review the Word List below for "Hound Dog Takes the Job."

mouse	*loud*	*about*	*hound*	*around*	*out*	*found*
pouted	*proud*	*arouse*	*straw*	*paw*	*yawn*	*animals*

b. Read this passage with your student.

> *That day, Hound Dog did not sleep. He kept the mice away. There was not a mouse to be found.*

Ask your student to find the word *mouse* and circle it. Ask him how many of these animals does the word *mouse* mean. **one** Ask him to find the word that means more than one mouse and underline it. **mice**

We have learned that many times we add the letter **s** to the end of a word when we mean more than one, such as one dog and five dogs. In some words, like *mouse*, we must change the word to mean more than one.

Ask your student to tell you the word to use in these blanks. This is an oral activity.

There is one *woman* at the desk and three ___*women*___ at the counter.
There is one *child* here and five ___*children*___ there.
I called one *man* and ended up talking to three ___*men*___.

c. Read the story *The Bravest Dog Ever* by Natalie Standiford with or to your student.

d. Talk with your student about the events of the story. Tell him about different types of stories: fiction (made-up stories) and nonfiction (true events). Discuss the story with your student.

   1) *Do you think this is fiction or nonfiction?* **Nonfiction**
   2) *What did you like about this story? Why?* **Answers will vary.**
   3) *Was there anything you didn't like about the story? Tell me more about that.*
     Answers will vary.
   4) *How do you feel about Balto? Do you think he was a hero? Why or why not?*
     Allow for discussion.

e. Find page 103 in the *Student Activity Book*. This is a map of Alaska. Ask your student to follow your directions on the map. Repeat them several times, as needed.

   1) *Use a red marker or pencil to show this path: the train left Anchorage, Point A on the map, and went north to Point N.*
   2) *Use a green marker or pencil to show this path: a dog sled picked up the medicine at the train, and took it west to Point T.*
   3) *Use a blue marker to show this path: several dog teams took the medicine west through Point R, Point K, south to Point L, west to Point H, Point G and Point B.*
   4) *Use an orange marker to show this path: Gunnar picked up the medicine at Point B and took it to Point S. There was no one at Point S, so Balto led the team on to Nome.*

Use an atlas, globe, or map to show your student where Alaska is compared to your home state. Now, show him New York City, where Balto's statue is located. Compare that location to Alaska. Ask your student to tell this true story about Balto, using his map.

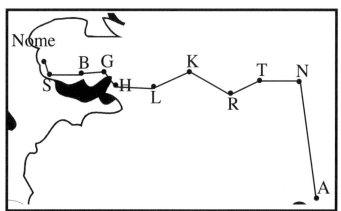

f. Help your student number a piece of paper 1 - 4. Dictate the spelling words to your student. If he has any difficulty at all, use the same process used in **2f**.

g. Find page 100 in the *Student Activity Book* and ask your student to copy the sentence on the bottom line and color the page. He may take two days to complete this assignment.

Day 5

a. Ask your student to read "Hound Dog Takes the Job" aloud. Celebrate his success and add to his Reading Chart.

b. Discuss real and make-believe stories with your student. Tell him that this week, we have read two stories about dogs, Hound Dog and Balto. Ask him which one was real and which one was make-believe, and why he thinks that.

c. Find page 105 in the *Student Activity Book*. Ask your student to cut out the boxes and put the real animals in one pile and the make-believe ones in another pile. Ask him to match the real bear and the make-believe bear, and to do the same with the fish and parrot.

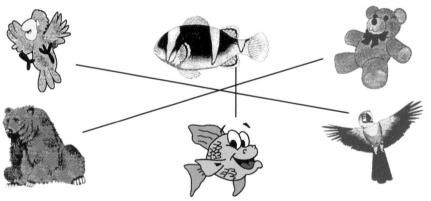

Ask your student to choose one pair of the animals. Ask him to make a book and glue the real animal on one page and the make-believe animal on another page. Ask him to write or dictate two to three sentences that tell what the real animals can do and two to three sentences that tell what the make-believe animal can do. This can be a short story or just a few sentences.

d. Look through books in your classroom or library, and ask your student to identify several nonfiction and fiction books. Find an old favorite and read it together.

Teacher's Note: This is a good opportunity to visit the library.

e. Optional: Spelling test

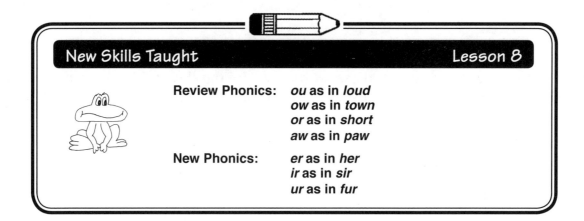

Review Phonics:　*ou* as in *loud*
　　　　　　　　　　　ow as in *town*
　　　　　　　　　　　or as in *short*
　　　　　　　　　　　aw as in *paw*

New Phonics:　　*er* as in *her*
　　　　　　　　　　ir as in *sir*
　　　　　　　　　　ur as in *fur*

Day 1

Materials needed:
All Around the Farm

a. Find the story, "Cat Visits the Town," in the reader, *All Around the Farm*. Read it to or with your student. Stop at the end of page 27 and ask your student what he thinks will happen next. Finish reading the story.

b. Discuss the story with your student.

1) *Did it end like you thought it might end?*
2) *Tell me the story in your own words.*
3) *What do you remember about Cat from our last story?* **She wanted to be a town cat.**
4) *Why do you think she thought she had to leave the farm?*
5) *Describe Prissy Cat.*
6) *What happens at the end of the story? Why do you think Cat heads home? What will Cat do now?*
7) *Does this story remind you of another story we read this year?* **"The Country Mouse's Big Adventure"**

c. Read this passage with your student.

　　Cat waved to Prissy. Prissy saw Cat running all the way home.

Ask your student to find the word that ends with **-ing** and circle it. The word *run* is spelled **r-u-n**, but *running* is spelled **r-u-n-n-i-n-g.**

Ask your student if he knows why the letter **n** is doubled before adding the **-ing**. One-syllable words which end with one short vowel and one consonant, must double its last consonant before adding **-ing** or **-ed**.

Help your student add **-ing** to these words by copying the words, doubling the last consonant, and then adding **-ing**: run - **running**, hop - **hopping**, stop - **stopping**, clap - **clapping**, sit - **sitting**.

Read the new words to or with your student.

d. Ask your student to say the words in the Phonics Word Box and put an X next to the sentence that best describes the picture: *found, town, corner, saw, farm, porch, throw*.

    ____1) The boys found a ball on the farm.
    ____2) We went to town and got a new mitt.
    _X_3) They will throw the ball to each other all day.
    ____4) I sat on the corner of the porch to read.

e. Ask your student to copy the spelling words for this week. Read them to or with your student: *paw with straw your*.

Day 2

a. Review the story for this week with your student.

b. Discuss Cat with your student.

1) *Cat was sure that she would like the town better than the farm. So sure, that she let all the farm animals down and refused to do her job. Why do you think she was so sure?*
2) *What made her change her mind?*
3) *How do you think Cat feels now? How would you feel if you were Cat?*

c. Beside the picture of Prissy, ask your student to write or dictate two to three sentences about the life of a town cat. Beside Cat, ask him to write or dictate two to three sentences about the life of a farm cat. Ask him which life sounds best to him and why.

d. How Do You Spell That Word?

Give your student a piece of paper. You will dictate the spelling words to him guiding him through the process by helping him with spelling rules. Read the following sections that your student needs to correctly spell the words.

The sound /aw/ as in claw *is spelled with* **aw** *at the end of a word.*

1) *paw - Since the /aw/ sound is at the end of the word, it is spelled* **aw**.
2) *with - This is a common word. If you do not remember, I will spell it for you.*

3) *straw* - If needed, use the rule from 1.
4) *your* - If needed, repeat from 2.

e. Find page 115 in the *Student Activity Book*. Ask your student to cut out the word cards for **2e** and put the suffix rules in a row. Then read each word card and decide which rule to use for that word, and tell him to put the word under the correct rule.
Just add -ed - kick   jump   call
Double the last consonant - stop   drop   hop   rip
Drop the e - smile poke bake

f. Tell your student that **er**, **ir**, and **ur** make the **/er/** sound. Read this passage with your student.

> *Cat sent a letter to Prissy Cat. The letter said, "It is urgent that I visit you. I must depart from farm life."*
> *Cat waited at her door. At last, Cat got a letter back from Prissy. Prissy said to come visit now. Cat made some firm plans. She would leave on the first bus to town.*

Ask your student to circle all the words with **er**, **ir**, or **ur**. Say the words and ask him to repeat after you. Remind him that these letter combinations say **/er/**.
her   letter   urgent   firm   first

Ask your student to look through the whole story and find five more **/er/** words.
Possible answers: corner, Third, fir, curls, hurting, better, under, ferns, surprised, curve, dirt, nerves, hurry, turned, other, returned, her, hurt

g. Find page 113 in the *Student Activity Book* and ask your student to complete it.

Day 3

a. Review the story for this week.

b. Read this passage with your student.

> *"Why can't we go inside the house?" asked Cat.*
> *"You silly cat. I do not live* inside *the house. I live under the porch."*

Remind your student that a compound word is two words joined together to make a new word. Ask him to circle the compound word which is used twice in this passage. **inside**

Find page 115 in the *Student Activity Book*, and ask him to read and cut out the word boxes for **3b**. He can combine them to make compound words. After you check the compound words, ask him to glue them on paper.

c. Context Words: *beautiful other door*. Read the words with your student. Ask him to read the sentences, using context clues as needed.

1) I like the blue coat, but I want the *other* one.
2) We were late for the show. I ran to the *doo*r and yelled, "Come on!"
3) That looks nice on you. It is a *beautiful* dress.

d. Syllable Sense

Remind your student that the first syllable of a word ends with a vowel, the vowel will usually say its long sound. Ex: **re / main**
Ask your student to divide these words. **1) re / turn   2) de / part   3) a / round**

Teacher's Note: Some students may say *around* with *a* short a sound. This is acceptable.

Tell your student that sometimes we add a letter or letters at the beginning of words. These are called prefixes. Two common prefixes are **re-** and **de-**.

Ask him to read these words: *repeat delay redo depart*.

e. Find page 111 in the *Student Activity Book* and make the two Word Family Flip Books. Ask your student to read the words to you. Give help as needed.

staple	_ing s	_ing th	_ang s	_ang b
	_ing str	_ing w	_ang cl	_ang f
	_ing br	_ing wr	_ang h	_ang r
	_ing r	_ing sw	_ang sl	
staple		ing (staple)	ang

sing	**thing**	**sang**	**bang**
string	**wing**	**clang**	**fang**
bring	**wring**	**hang**	**rang**
ring	**swing**	**slang**	

f. Ask your student to complete the Spelling Words Puzzle.

1) with   2) straw   3) paw   4) your

g. Find page 114 in the *Student Activity Book* and ask him to trace the sentence on the top of the page.

Day 4

4. a. Review the Word List below for "Cat Visits the Town."

letter	*corner*	*under*	*better*	*nerves*	*firm*	*first*
third	*dirt*	*urgent*	*curls*	*hurt*	*beautiful*	

b. Read this passage with your student.

> *"You silly cat. I do not live inside the house. I live under the porch," said Prissy.*
> *"I see," said Cat. She was surprised. "Where do you sleep?"*
> *"I sleep in the ferns under the porch," said Prissy.*

Ask your student how many characters are speaking in this passage. **two** Tell him that the quotation marks tell us someone is speaking. The words inside the quotation marks are the exact words spoken. Ask him to underline the exact words that Prissy says in the passage. **You silly cat. I do not live inside the house. I live under the porch. I sleep in the ferns under the porch.** Circle the exact words that Cat says in the passage.

⟨ **I see. Where do you sleep?** ⟩

Ask your student to read the exact words of Prissy while you read Cat's words. Encourage him to use expression in his voice as he reads.

c. Find page 117 in the *Student Activity Book*. Ask your student to look at the picture and tell you what he sees. Today, your student will begin a story about this picture. Spend plenty of time talking to him before he begins the story. You may use the following questions to help you in your discussion.

1) *Whose party is it? Tell me about her.*
2) *What special people are at the party?*
3) *What special activities will they do at the party?*
4) *Look at the special decorations. Who put those up?*
5) *How does the birthday person feel at the party?*

On a separate piece of paper, ask your student to write the rough draft of his story, or dictate it to you. Encourage him to use the activity from **2e** for any words with the suffix**-ing**. Make this an enjoyable activity for your student. Do not push him to make it more than he wants it to be. Help your student edit the story. On Day 5, your student will write the final copy on the lines below the picture.

d. Help your student number a piece of paper 1 - 4. Dictate the spelling words to your student. If he has any difficulty at all, use the same process used in **2d**.

e. Find page 114 in the *Student Activity Book* and ask your student to copy the sentence on the bottom line and color the page. He may take two days to complete this assignment.

Day 5

a. Ask your student to read "Cat Visits the Town" aloud. Celebrate his success and add to his Reading Chart.

b. Today, your student will write the final copy of the story from **4c.** Ask him to color the picture and write the story under the picture.

Read the story with your student. If he is pleased with it, ask him to read it or tell it to a group, showing the picture as he presents the story.

c. Find page 119 in the *Student Activity Book*. Ask your student to decorate the card and give it to someone. It can be a birthday card or a friendship card. He can write or dictate the message inside the card.

d. Optional: Spelling test

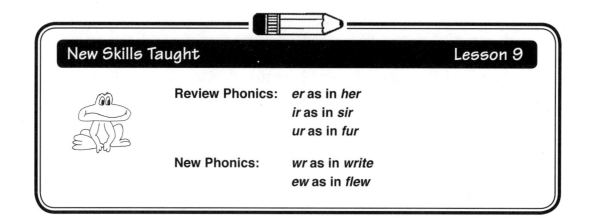

New Skills Taught　　　　　　　　　　　　　**Lesson 9**

Review Phonics: *er* as in *her*
　　　　　　　　　　ir as in *sir*
　　　　　　　　　　ur as in *fur*

New Phonics:　　*wr* as in *write*
　　　　　　　　　　ew as in *flew*

Day 1

a. Find the story, "Cat was Wrong," from the reader, *All Around the Farm*. Read it to or with your student.

b. Discuss the story with your student.

　　1) *Tell me the story in your own words.* **Self-explanatory**
　　2) *What important lesson did Cat learn in our last story?* **Home was better.**
　　3) *Why is Cat afraid to tell the other animals that she was wrong?* **She's afraid they will laugh at her.** *Have you ever felt that way?* **Answers will vary.**
　　4) *Why do you think Hound Dog is glad to see Cat back on the farm?* **Possible answers: He liked Cat. He was tired of chasing mice. He wanted to play.**
　　5) *How would you tell this story from Hound Dog's point of view?* **Possible answer: I was doing my best to keep the mice away. But I missed Cat. Then one day she came home. I was so happy.**

c. Ask your student to tell you the number of syllables in these words: *concern　return　hurray*. Remind your student of the two syllable rules we have learned.

Divide the word between the two consonants in the middle of the word. Ex: bat/tle un/til When the word has a vowel, consonant, vowel, divide the word after the first vowel. Ex: be/tween

Ask your student to draw a line to divide the words and say them aloud. **1) con/cern　2) re/turn　3) hur/ray**

　　d. Ask your student to look through storybooks or other school books and find four words that follow each syllable rule. He may show them to you or write them on paper.

Materials needed:
　All Around the Farm

　The Fire Cat by Esther Averill

e. Ask your student to read the words in the Phonics Word Boxes and write the correct word in the sentence blank:

under   bird   stir
over   shore

1) The **bird** flew to the tree.
2) The boat floated **under** the bridge.
3) We played at the sea **shore**.
4) We walked **over** the bridge.
5) Will you **stir** the cake mix?

turn   sharp   torn
nurse   party

6) Please **turn** left at the light.
7) The **nurse** gave me a shot.
8) The needle felt **sharp**.
9) Can you sew my **torn** coat?
10) I went to a birthday **party**.

f. Ask your student to copy the spelling words for this week. Read them to or with your student: *dirty hurt under herd*.

Day 2

a. Review the story for this week.

b. Discuss Cat with your student.

1) *Cat is sad at the beginning of the story. How does she feel at the end of the story?* **She is happy to be chasing mice again.**
2) *Part of the reason she feels happy at the end is because she has her job back. What is another reason?* **She has apologized to the animals and has been forgiven**.
3) *Was it hard for Cat to do the right thing in this story? Why or why not?* **Allow for discussion.**
4) *Have you ever had to do something that was the right thing, but it was hard to do? Tell me about it.* **Allow for discussion.**

c. Read this passage with your student.

> *"I was wrong about the town. I was wrong to leave the farm. I love it here. I am sorry I quit my job. Will you forgive me?" Cat said. She hung her head down.*

Ask your student to find a word in the passage that is made up of two words and circle it. **forgive** Find page 127 in the *Student Activity Book* and ask your student to cut out the boxes for **2c**. Read each word with him. Ask him to put each word with another word to make a new compound word.

somewhere	**someone**	**something**	**herself**	**himself**
yourself	**forgive**	**forget**	**forgot**	

d. How Do You Spell That Word?

Give your student a piece of paper. Dictate the spelling words guiding him through the process by helping him with spelling rules. Read the following sections that your student needs to correctly spell the words.

The sound /er/ as in her *can be spelled many ways. The three most common ways are* **er**, **ur**, *and* **ir**. *Can you remember which one to use in these words?*
1) *under*
2) *dirty*
3) *herd*
4) *hurt*

e. Reread the passage from **2c** with your student. In the passage, there is a word that begins with the letters **wr**, but we do not hear the **w** when we say the word. Ask your student to find this word and circle it. Tell your student that the letter combination **wr** sounds like /**r**/. Ask him to read these words: *write, wrote, wrap, wreck, wrist.*

f. Find page 125 in the *Student Activity Book* and ask your student to complete it.

Day 3

a. Review the story for this week.

b. Read this passage with your student.

> *Mama Cow spoke first, "I will forgive you. I missed you, Cat. I am glad you are back."*

Tell your student that Mama Cow uses a little word to mean herself. Ask him to find it and circle it. **I** Mama Cow also uses another word to mean Cat. Ask him to find that word. **you** These little words are called pronouns. Pronouns replace a naming word, or noun, so we do not have to use the same word over and over. Ask your student what pronoun can replace the underlined noun.

1) <u>Alice</u> rode the bike. **She**
2) <u>Jim</u> ran to the store. **He**

Read this passage to your student.

> *Cat looked up at the animals. She saw a few harsh looks but more smiles. Cat gave them a smile.*

There is a pronoun that takes the place of *animals* in the last sentence of the passage. Ask your student to find and circle it. **them**

Ask your student to listen to these sentences, and circle the pronoun. Ask him to tell you or write the noun it replaces.
Ex: *Sally said, "I will fix the cake."*   ***Sally* replaces the pronoun *I*.**

3) The family had a picnic. (They) ate chicken and rolls. ***They* replaces *the family*.**
4) Bill said, "I will clean the car." ***I* replaces *Bill*.**
5) Mom said, "You can help, *Kate*." ***You* replaces *Kate*.**

c. Context Words: *guess most*. Read the words with your student. Ask him to read the sentences. Use context clues, as needed.

1) I see a few of the candy canes, but where are *most* of them?

Teacher's Note: Point out the contrast in *few* and *most*.

2) I do not want to work, but I *guess* I have to do it.

d. Read this passage with your student.

She saw a few harsh looks but more smiles.

Ask him how many harsh looks Cat saw when she looked at the animals. **few**
The **ew** in *few* says /ū/. The letters **ew** can also say /oo/ as in *grew*. Ask your student to say these **ew** words: *crew stew flew dew grew*.

Teacher's Note: *ew* says /ū/ as in *few* and /oo/ as in *grew*. The two sounds of *ew* are so similar, they are taught as one.

Ask him to look through the story and find any more **ew** words and read them to you.

e. Find page 127 in the *Student Activity Book* and make a Word Family Flip Book for **_ong**. Read the words with your student. Find the previously made Flip Books and review those words.

staple _ong s	_ong l	_ong wr
_ong str	_ong th	_ong b
	staple ong	

song	**long**	**wrong**
strong	**thong**	**bong**

f. Ask your student to write two rhyming lines on a separate piece of paper using words from any of the Word Family Flip Books.

> Ex: I found plenty of *string,*
>   On top of that *thing.*

He can illustrate each group of sentences to help it make sense or make it funny.

g. Ask your student to complete the Spelling Words Puzzle.
   1) herd 2) under 3) hurt 4) dirty

h. Find page 126 in the *Student Activity Book* and ask him to trace the sentence on the top of the page.

Day 4

a. Review the Word List below for "Cat Was Wrong."

new	*few*	*blew*	*wrong*	*started*	*harsh*
most	*guess*	*concern*	*returned*	*hurray*	

b. Ask your student to read each of the following sentences to you and choose the correct pronoun to replace the words.

1) *Mom* is going to the store. **She**   2) *Dad and I* are playing ball. **We**
3) *Mom and Dad* love me. **They**   4) *Dad* is going to the game. **He**

c. Read the book, *The Fire Cat*, by Esther Averill to or with your student. Stop at the end of each story and discuss what has happened and what your student thinks will happen next. At the end of the book, discuss the story with your student.

1) *Pickles wanted to do big things in his life. Did he do that? Yes, explain how he did.* **He became a fire cat.**

2) *How is Pickles like Cat, from All Around the Farm?* **Both are cats, and they want to be something different than what they are at the beginning of the stories.**

3) *How is Pickles different from Cat?* **Pickles' ideas about himself came true; Cat's ideas of being a town cat did not happen. Pickles worked hard to be a fire cat; Cat decided she did not want to be a town cat.**

d. Ask your student to draw Cat and Pickles on a separate sheet of paper. Ask him to write two to three sentences under each picture telling what he likes about this character and what, if anything, he did not like about him. Be sure to discuss why he thinks this way.

e. Help your student number a piece of paper 1 - 4. Dictate the spelling words to your student. If he has any difficulty at all, use the same process used in **2d**.

f. Find page 126 in the *Student Activity Book* and ask your student to copy the sentence on the bottom line and color the page. He may take two days to complete this assignment.

Day 5

a. Ask your student to read the story, "Cat was Wrong," aloud. Celebrate his success and add to his Reading Chart.

b. Tell your student that you are going to do what is called "pantomime." Please look up the word in a dictionary if you have questions about what it means. Using only actions, and not words, ask him to show what he would do if he were: happy scared tired sad loving mad.

c. Ask your student to read each sentence on page 129 of the *Student Activity Book*, **5c**. Ask him to look at each picture and decide which picture matches the sentence. Ask him to copy the sentence beside the correct picture. Show him the example on the page. **1) I need to sleep. 2) I like to sing. 3) What a sad story. 4) A gift for me!**

d. Using the **5c** activity as an example, on a seperate piece of paper, ask your student to draw a picture and write or dictate a short sentence for it. Remind him to use a capital letter at the beginning of the sentence and use the correct end mark at the end of the sentence.

e. Optional: Spelling test

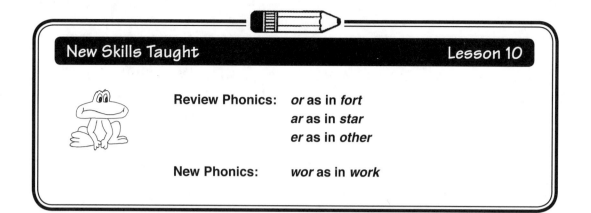

Review Phonics: *or* as in *fort*
                          ar as in *star*
                          er as in *other*

New Phonics: *wor* as in *work*

Day 1

a. Find the story, "The Best Work in the World," in the reader, *All Around the Farm*. Read it to or with your student.

b. Discuss the story with your student.

   1) *Tell me the story in your own words.* **Self-explanatory**
   2) *What is Hound Dog's worry?* **He had no work.** *Who decides to help him?* **Pig and the other animals help him.** *How do they help him?* **They told Farmer that he is a smart dog.**
   3) *Farmer gives Hound Dog a chance at herding the sheep. How would you describe Hound Dog as a worker?* **He is a good worker.**

c. Read this passage with your student.

> *Hound Dog bounded up the hill with Farmer. He barked and made the sheep hurry up. Hound Dog stayed with the herd until dark.*
> *Farmer patted Hound Dog. He said, "You are a smart sheep dog."*
> *Hound Dog smiled at his owner. "It is hard work, but it is the best work in the world."*

Tell your student that this passage contains several action words, or words that tell what a character is doing in the story. Ask him to find as many as he can and circle them. **bounded, barked, made, stayed, patted, said, smiled**.

Materials needed:
   All Around the Farm

   craft materials

✎ **Teacher's Note:** Being verbs and helping verbs will be taught in a higher level book.

One way to find the action word is to ask the question "What did he do?" So, for the first sentence of the passage, you can ask,"*What did Hound Dog do?*" Hound Dog *bounded*. Your student may say that Hound Dog *bounded up the hill*. That is fine for now. Ask him to circle only the action word. Continue with the questions on any action verbs he did not circle.

d. Ask your student to act out these action words: *jump laugh smile growl sit stomp*.

e. Review these three sounds with your student: **er** says /**er**/ as in *her*, **ar** says /**ar**/ as in *car*, and **or** says /**or**/ as in *fort*. Read the following words to your student, and ask him to tell you the sound he hears in the word: *port* - **or**; *star* - **ar**; *mother* - **er**; *garden* - **ar**; *park* - **ar**; *fern* - **er**; *sport* - **or**; *danger* - **er**; *jar* - **ar**; *born* - **or**; *cork*- **or**; *other* - **er**.

After you have finished, ask your student to write each word in the correct column as you read them again.

f. Ask your student to copy the spelling words for this week. Read them to or with your student: *new said there blew*.

Day 2

a. Review the story for this week with your student.

b. Read this passage with your student.

> *The next morning, Farmer came into the barn. Cow said, "Hound Dog is a good worker." Farmer just listened.*
> *Then Farmer led Goat out to the barnyard. Goat said, "Farmer, Hound Dog did a good job with the mice." Farmer just listened.*
> *The chickens said, "Hound Dog does not look like much on the outside, but he is a smart dog." Farmer just listened.*

Ask your student to find the word which Cow used to tell what kind of worker Hound Dog is and circle it. **good** Ask him to think of another word that means almost the same as *good* and could be used to replace *good* in this sentence. **Possible answers: fine, hard, great** Tell him that words with the same or almost the same meaning are called synonyms. Use a thesaurus if one is available. Use this time to show your student how a **thesaurus** lists words in alphabetical order, and how it is used to find **synonyms** (words of similar meaning) and **antonyms** (words of opposite meaning). Ask your student to find and circle the word which Goat used to describe the job Hound Dog did with the mice. ***good*** job What word did the chickens use to tell what kind of dog he is now. *smart* **dog** Ask him to find a synonym for each of these describing words. **Possible answers: good: fine great proper decent smart: bright wise clever intelligent**

c. Ask your student to find synonyms for the words: *next came look led said.* Using these synonyms and the synonyms he found for *good* and *smart*, read the passage in **2b** using them in place of the listed words.

   Possible answers:
   1) next - **following**   2) came - **walked, strolled**   3) look - **appear**
   4) led - **took**   5) said - **explained, whispered**

d. Reread the passage from **2b** with your student. Tell him that we have learned that **or** usually says **/or/** as in *fort*. In this passage, there is a word with **or**, but it does not say **/or/**. Ask him to find it and underline it. **worker**

   Wor says **/wer/** as in *word*. Ask him if he can find five more **wor** words in the story. **worry, work, word, worthy, world**

   Ask your student to read the words in the Phonics Word Box: *worry, work, word, worthy, world.*

e. How Do You Spell That Word?

   Give your student a piece of paper. Dictate the spelling words guiding him through the process by helping him with spelling rules. Read the following sections that your student needs to correctly spell the words.

   1) *new - The /oo/ sound at the end of a word is often spelled **ew**.*
   2) *said - This is a common word; if you don't remember how to spell it, I will tell you.*
   3) *blew - If needed, use rule from 1.*
   4) *there - If needed, use statement from 2.*

f. Find page 135 in the *Student Activity Book* and ask your student to complete it.

Day 3

a. Review the story for this week.

b. The story this week is about Hound Dog's new job. Read this sentence with your student.

> *This week, we read about Hound Dog's new job.*

Ask your student to find the word with the apostrophe **s** ('**s**) at the end of it and circle it. Tell him this shows that the job belongs to Hound Dog. On page 133 of the *Student Activity Book* are two columns labeled, *Things That Belong To Teacher - Things That Belong To* _____. Ask your student to write his name in the blank.

Make a list of three things that belong to each person. Ex: Mom's purse; Nathan's bat

Use the apostrophe and **s** at the end of the person's name to show that something belongs to them. If needed, remind your student to begin the name with a capital letter.

Teacher's Note: If the teacher's or student's name ends with an s, just add an apostrophe. This will be taught in a higher level book.

c. Remind your student that we use an apostrophe in another type of word. When we combine two words to make a shortened form of those words, sometimes we leave out letters. When we leave out letters, we put in an apostrophe. Ex: can + not = can't We left out the letters **n** and **o** and put in an apostrophe.

Find page 139 in the *Student Activity Book* and ask your student to cut out the word cards for **3c**. Ask your student to use a pencil to mark out the letters we would take out to make these words contractions. After you have checked it, ask him to cut out those letters and glue the rest of them on blank paper, adding the apostrophe to make a list of contractions.

can't   isn't   I've   It's   I'll   don't   We've   you've   you'll

d. Your student may use the contractions from **3c** to complete these sentences. Remind him that sentences start with capital letters.

1) Mom **can't** pick up the big box.
2) This **isn't** the way to the store.
3) **I've** got a new boat.
4) **It's** blue and white.
5) **I'll** wait for you outside.
6) We **don't** have any bait for fishing.
7) **We've** got a new pet at home.
8) **You've** got to go home now.
9) I hope **you'll** come.

e. Context Words: *listened   always*. Read the words with your student. Ask your student to read the sentences and use context clues.

1) We never go to the mall, but we *always* go to the bookstore.
2) I talked to my dad. He *listened* to me for a long time.

f. Ask your student to complete the Spelling Words Puzzle.
1) new   2) blew   3) there   4) would

g. Find page 136 in the *Student Activity Book* and ask him to trace the sentence on the top of the page.

Day 4

4. a. Review the Word List below for "The Best Work in the World."

worry	*work*	*word*	*worthy*	*world*
listened	*always*	*owner*	*gathered*	

b. Look through *All Around the Farm* with your student. Talk about the characters, stories, and setting. Discuss it with your student.

1) *Which characters do you like? Why?*
2) *Which stories do you like? Why?*
3) *What do you like about the pictures?*
4) Show your student the title page and read the title, author, illustrator, and publisher. *Do you know what the author did for this book?* **She wrote the book.** *What did the illustrator do for this book?* **She drew the pictures.** *What did the publisher do for this book?* **He had the book printed and sent it to the stores so we could buy it.**
5) Show your student the copyright page and table of contents. *The copyright page tells you more about the book and the publisher. It also tells us we cannot copy this book and sell or give it someone. The table of contents tell us on what page each story begins.*

c. Find page 139 in the *Student Activity Book*. There are several pictures of the characters and objects from *All Around the Farm* for **4c**. Discuss these Farm Project ideas with your student and ask him to choose a project to work on today and tomorrow.

    1) Color and cut out pictures. Use a shoe box and create a 3-D scene, or diorama, of the farm. Your student can write or dictate a summary of a few stories from the reader or make up his own.

    2) Color and cut out pictures. Create a sentence about six of the pictures. Glue the pictures on the top of a piece of paper and write the sentence under each picture.

    3) Create a new story about our farm friends. Color and cut out the pictures. Make a book by stapling several pages together. Write the story in the book, and glue the pictures as desired.

d. Help your student number a piece of paper 1 - 4. Dictate the spelling words to your student. If he has any difficulty at all, use the same process used in **2e**.

e. Find page 136 in the *Student Activity Book* and ask your student to copy the sentence on the bottom line and color the page. He may take two days to complete this assignment.

Day 5

5. a. Ask your student to read the story, "The Best Work in the World," aloud. Celebrate his success and add to his Reading Chart. Your student has read the book, *All Around the Farm*. Add the book cover to his Reading Chart.

   b. Continue work on the Farm Project.

   c. Prepare to present it to a group.

   d. Optional: Spelling test

   e. Complete *Assessment 2* with your student.

Assessment 2
(Lessons 5 - 10)

This is the oral part of *Assessment 2*.

1. *There are three kinds of sentences.*

    a. *Tell me a sentence that asks a question.* **Answers will vary.**
       What punctuation ends an asking sentence? **a question mark**

    b. *Tell me a sentence that shows strong feeling.* **Answers will vary.**
       What punctuation ends this kind of sentence? **an exclamation mark**

    c. *Tell me a sentence that just tells something.* **Answers will vary.**
       What punctuation ends a telling sentence? **a period**

2. *An adjective is a word that describes a noun, or naming word.*

    a. *Tell me an adjective to describe your hair.* **Possible answers: straight, curly, long, short, brown**
    b. *Tell me an adjective to describe something you see around you.* **Answers will vary.**

3. *Synonyms are words that have the same or almost the same meaning. Tell me a synonym for these words as I use them in sentences.*

    a. *happy*   *The little boy was happy to see his father.* **Possible answers: glad, joyful, ecstatic, jubilant**
    b. *ran*   *The mouse ran across the room.* **Possible answers: scurried, went, tiptoed**

4. *Contractions are a shortened way of saying two words together. For example,* wouldn't *is a contraction for* would not. *Tell me the words for these contractions as I use them in sentences.*

    a. *I'll*   *I'll go home.* **I will**
    b. *isn't*   *Mom isn't home.* **is not**

5. *Words are usually made plural, to mean more than one of something, by just adding* **s**. *For example, one dog and two dogs. Some words change when they mean more than one, such as one child and two children. Tell me the plural for these words.*

    a. *one mouse* **two mice**
    b. *one man* **two men**

This is the written part of *Assessment 2*. Ask your student to find page 138 in the *Student Activity Book*, and ask him to complete it as you instruct him.

1. *Add* **-ed** *to these words.*

    a. help **helped**
    b. fan **fanned**
    c. hike **hiked**

2. *Homonyms are words that often sound the same but have a different meaning and usually a different spelling. Look at your sentences as I read to you. Circle the correct word.*

    a. I **rode** my bike on the sidewalk.
    b. There were many cars on the **road**.
    c. I have **one** brother.
    d. He **won** the race.

3. *Look at your sentence as I read to you.*

  "Please walk the dog," said Dad.

  Tell me the actual words spoken by Dad. **Please walk the dog.** *How did you know?*
  (oral answer) The words inside the quotation marks are the actual words spoken.

4. *Look at your sentence as I read to you.*

  Where is the baby's blanket?

  How do you know who owns the blanket? **(oral answer)**
  The apostrophe and s tells us that the blanket belongs to the baby.

  Ask your student to complete these sentences with apostrophes.

    a. *The mans car is blue.* **The man's car is blue.**
    b. *This is your sisters hot dog.* **This is your sister's hot dog.**

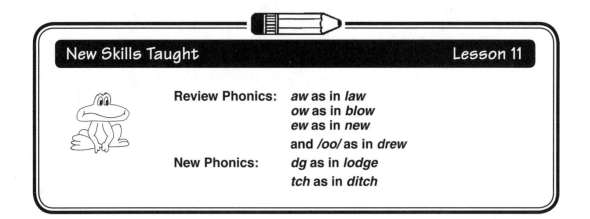

New Skills Taught   **Lesson 11**

Review Phonics:	*aw* as in *law*	
	ow as in *blow*	
	ew as in *new*	
	and */oo/* as in *drew*	
New Phonics:	*dg* as in *lodge*	
	tch as in *ditch*	

Day 1

Materials needed:
Forest Fables

stationery and envelope

a. Find the story, "A Stitch in Time," in the reader, *Forest Fables*. Read it to or with your student.

b. Discuss the story with your student.

1) *Tell me the story in your own words.*
2) *Badger was in a big hurry to get to Hedgehog's house. Why do you think she was in such a hurry?*
3) *Badger did not want to stop and take time to sew on one button. Was that a wise decision? Why or why not?*
4) *How much time do you think it would take to sew on one button on a jacket? How much time do you think it would take to sew on nine buttons?*

c. Read this passage with your student.

    Badger looked at her watch. "That will take so much time," Badger said. "If I had just stitched the one button when it was first falling off, I would have saved time. Now, I must stitch all nine buttons. Next time, I will remember this truth: A stitch in time saves nine."

In the last sentence, there is a word with three syllables in it. Ask your student to find that word and circle it. If your student has trouble counting syllables, remind him to clap for each sound he hears in the word. **remember**

Teacher's Note: The last sentence begins *Next time... nine*.

81

Find page 143 in the *Student Activity Book*. Ask your student to cut out all the word boxes for **1c** and line the *1 Syllable Card*, *2 Syllables Card*, and the *3 Syllables Card* in a row. Read a word card with your student and ask him to place it under the correct title. Continue until they are all in a row. Glue these word cards on paper.

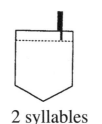

1 syllable	2 syllables	3 syllables
door want late six shoe	**seven very little open**	**somebody important faraway**

d. Ask your student to use the sheet from **1c** and write or dictate one sentence with a word from each row on a separate piece of paper. Ex: That is an important little shoe.

e. Review these sounds with your student: **aw** says /aw/ as in *saw*, **ow** says /ō/ as in *blow*, and **ew** says /oo/ as in *drew* or /u/ as in *new*. Have the student cut out the word cards for **1e** on page 143. On a piece of paper, glue the sound clue cards on the top in a row. Read each word card with your student and have him glue it under the correct column.
aw says /aw/ - claw paw saw straw law
ow says /ō/ - mow show blow crow bow
ew says /oo/ or /ū/ - chew blew grew new few

f. Ask your student to copy the spelling words for this week. Read them to or with your student: *third worry word first*.

Day 2

a. Review the story for this week with your student.

b. Find page 145 in the *Student Activity Book*. Talk to your student about each picture. Ask him to cut out the pictures for **2b** and put them in the correct order. He can use the story if needed.

c. Tell the student to glue each picture onto a separate piece of paper, and write a sentence about it below. Remind him that in our story, Badger and Hedgehog are these animal's particular names, so they are proper nouns and need to be capitalized. When he is finished, arrange the pages in order and staple them together to form a book.

d. Remind your student of the rules we have learned about adding the suffixes **-ed** and **-ing** to a word. Ask your student to look through the story and find at least one word for each rule listed.

Just add -ed/-ing	Drop silent e and add -ed/-ing	Double the consonant and add -ed/-ing
stitched, looked	liked	stopped
falling, handed	saved	ripping
lifted		tapped
thanked		

e. How Do You Spell That Word?

Give your student a piece of paper. You will dictate the spelling words to him guiding him through the process by helping him with spelling rules. Read the following sections that your student needs to correctly spell the words.

The **/er/** sound can be spelled many ways. The most common way of spelling the **/er/** sound is **er, ir,** or **ur**. If a word begins with a **w** and then **/er/**, it is usually spelled **wor**.

1) *word - Since the /er/ sound follows the w at the beginning of the word, the word is spelled* **wor**.
2) *third - The /er/ sound is usually spelled with* **-er, -ir,** *or* **-ur**. Tell your student if he does not know.
3) *first - If needed, use the rule for 2.*
4) *worry - If needed, use the rule for 1.*

f. Read this passage with your student.

> *Badger got a new coat. It had two pockets and nine shiny buttons. She put on her coat. Badger liked her new coat. She buttoned all nine buttons. The last button was falling off. "The button is not off yet. I will stitch it later," said Badger. Now, she was ready for tea with Hedgehog.*

Ask your student to circle the names of the two characters in this passage. **Badger and Hedgehog** Each name has the letter combination **dg**. What sound does he hear in those letters? **/j/ sound** Point out the word *stitch*. Ask your student what sound **tch** makes in this word. **/ch/ sound** Ask your student to use the clues to read this list of words in the Phonics Word Box to you: *edge ledge ridge fudge wedge watch match itch pitch kitchen.*

g. Find page 151 in the *Student Activity Book* and ask your student to complete it.

Day 3

a. Review the story for this week with your student.

b. Ask your student if he has ever heard the expression: *A stitch in time saves nine.* What does he think it means? Ask your student if he can think of anything in his life where this proverb will help him.

   Ex: If you do not take time to brush your teeth, you may have to spend extra time and money at the dentist.

   Think of other ways this proverb is helpful and discuss them with your student.

 c. Find page 153 in the *Student Activity Book*. Ask your student to color it and find a good place to hang it up so everyone will remember this proverb. Explain that the X's are there to make it look like a cross-stitched or embroidered picture.

d. Context Words: *truth   where   both*. Use context clues to help your student read these words in these sentences.

   1) I have looked for my boots. Do you know *where* they are?
   2) I like the blue and the red one. I will take them *both*.
   3) It is a good idea to tell the *truth* all the time.

e. Remind your student that a pronoun takes the place of a noun. Read the pronouns with him. Ask him to fill in the blanks with the correct pronoun: *it he she they we I you*.

   1) *Tom and I* went to town. **We** wanted to see the circus.
   2) This *book* is mine. I will share **it** with you.
   3) *Sally* likes dogs. **She** has two of them.
   4) *Tom* likes cats. **He** has six of them.
   5) *Mom and Dad* like pizza. **They** want to eat some now.
   6) If this is your *book*, please put **it** on the shelf.

f. Ask your student to complete the Spelling Words Puzzle.
   1) word   2) third   3) first   4) worry

g. Find page 152 in the *Student Activity Book* and ask him to trace the sentence on the top of the page.

Day 4

a. Review the Word List below for "A Stitch in Time."

Badger	*Hedgehog*	*bridge*	*lodge*	*edge*	*fudge*
stitch	*match*	*watch*	*truth*	*where*	*remember*

b. Read Ecclesiastes 3:1-8 to your student. Talk with him about the cycles of life described in the Scripture. There are things that happen that make us sad, but they are a part of the normal course of life. Remind your student about the family tree he made in Lesson 1. Each generation adds many special things to a family.

Ecclesiastes 3:1-8   NASB

There is an appointed time for everything. And there is a
time for every event under heaven—
A time to give birth, and a time to die;
A time to plant, and a time to uproot what is planted.
A time to kill, and a time to heal;
A time to tear down, and a time to build up.
A time to weep, and a time to laugh;
A time to mourn, and a time to dance.
A time to throw stones, and a time to gather stones;
A time to embrace, and a time to shun embracing.
A time to search, and a time to give up as lost;
A time to keep, and a time to throw away.
A time to tear apart, and a time to sew together;
A time to be silent, and a time to speak.
A time to love, and a time to hate;
A time for war, and a time for peace.

c. Find page 155 in the *Student Activity Book* and help your student make his own address book of relatives and friends. Remind him that people's names need to begin with a capital letter. Help him write the addresses correctly, using capital letters and punctuation correctly. Show him how the book is put in alphabetical order. Explain to your student that if words or names are in alphabetical order, it is easier to find.

Ex: Jason Burke
123 Good Street
Denver, CO 97021

d. Using an atlas or map, show your student the location of special relatives not living in your town. Talk about their locale and how long it would take to get there. You may want to close the discussion with the thought that special people are worth making effort for, whether it's in the form of a visit, phone call, or letter.

e. Help your student number a piece of paper 1 - 4. Dictate the spelling words to your student. If he has any difficulty at all, use the same process used in **2e**.

f. Find page 152 in the *Student Activity Book* and ask your student to copy the sentence on the bottom line and color the page. He may take two days to complete this assignment.

Day 5

a. Ask your student to read the story, "A Stitch in Time," aloud. Celebrate his success and add to his Reading Chart.

b. Write today's date on paper or a board. Explain to your student that when we write a date, we write the name of the month, beginning with a capital letter, the date in the month, and the year. We separate the day of the month and year with a comma. Why do you think the comma is put there?

Ex: Monday, April 10, 1989

Practice writing today's date correctly, including the month, the date, and year. Write your birthday, including the year you were born. For the next week, write the date on your daily work.

c. Ask your student to look in his address book and choose someone to whom he would like to write a letter. Show him the parts of a letter: date, greeting, body, closing, and signature. You may want to add to the fun by mailing it, even it they live close by.

June 10, 1998 (*Date*)

Dear Grandma, (Greeting)

   (*Body*) Thank you very much for the book and toy. I like them very much. Tigers are my favorite.

Love, (*Closing*)
Bobby (*Signature*)

---

d. Help your student address the envelope and mail the letter.

Bobby Chung   STAMP
999 First Street
Seattle, WA 09621

                          Mrs. U.R. Grandma
                          123 Maple Road
                          Dallas, TX 86345

e. Optional: Spelling test

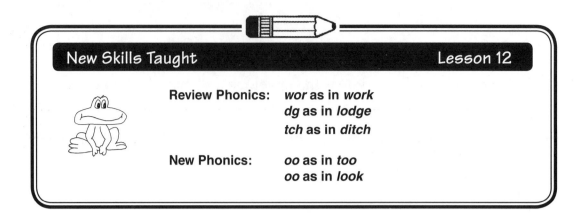

Review Phonics: *wor* as in *work*
                        dg as in *lodge*
                        tch as in *ditch*

New Phonics: *oo* as in *too*
                        oo as in *look*

Day 1

Materials Needed:
Forest Fables

✎ **Teacher's Note:** Your student is to write the date in the *Student Activity Book* everyday this week.

a. Find the story, "The Grass on the Other Side," in the reader, *Forest Fables*. Read it to or with your student.

b. Discuss the story with your student.

1) *Tell me the story in your own words.* **Self-explanatory**
2) *Can you tell me two reasons why Deer went on the other side of the brook?* **He was tired of his grass and he thought the other grass looked better.**
3) *What did Deer learn?* **The grass on the other side was the same.**
4) *Do you think Fawn will listen to Deer? Why or why not?* **Allow for discussion.**

c. Read this passage with your student.

> *Deer stared at the green grass on the other side of the brook. "If only I could eat that grass, I would be in a good mood." Deer made up his mind. He went to look for the greener grass. When he got to the other side, he started to eat the grass. He took only a few bites. He found that the grass did not taste so special.*

With your student, look at the sentence, "Deer made up his mind." We could say, "Deer made up *Deer's* mind," but that sounds funny.

Show your student that *Deer's mind* tells us that the mind belongs to *Deer*. Since we need another word to replace *Deer*, we use the pronoun *he* for *Deer* and make it show ownership by using the pronoun, *his*.

Here's another example: April gave me her book. The book belongs to April and *her* is an ownership pronoun or possessive pronoun that tells me that it is April's book. Read the possessive pronouns in the box with your student. Make sure he understands how a possessive pronoun is used. *his her hers their theirs its our ours your yours my mine*

Ask your student to read each sentence and circle the possessive pronoun. Have him draw a box around the name of the owner, and draw an arrow from the pronoun to the name.

Ex: [Dan and I] went to the store. The store is near (our) house.

1) [Jim] likes this book. The book is (his) favorite.

2) [Sally] gave me some of (her) cake.

3) [Jim and Sally] played (their) game.

4) [Mom and I] like the cake. The cake is (our) favorite.

d. Ask your student to write two to three sentences about a pet or item that is special to him, using at least one possessive pronoun.

e. Ask your student to read the words in the Phonics Word Box to you and fill in the blanks: *lodge edge ditch worth sketch worm.*

1) We used a **worm** to catch the fish.
2) Badger lived in a **lodge**.
3) I will **sketch** a picture of you.
4) That book is **worth** $5.00.
5) Beaver put a new dam on the **edge** of the river.
6) We had to dig a big **ditch**.

f. Ask your student to copy the spelling words for this week. Read them to or with your student: *fudge bridge match watch.*

Day 2

a. Review the story for this week with your student.

b. Discuss fact and opinion with your student. Emphasize to your student that a fact can be proven a number of times, and an opinion is someone's belief about something.

1) *What was Deer's opinion of his old grass?* **He was tired of it.**
2) *What was Rabbit's opinion of that same grass?* **It is green, cool, and yummy.**
3) *When Deer saw grass on the other side of the brook, what was his opinion of it?* **It must taste better because it looked greener.**
4) *Was it a fact that the grass on the other side was better tasting?* **No**

c. Read these sentences to your student. Ask him to tell you or write if it is a fact (F) or opinion (O).

   1) The earth moves around the sun. **F**
   2) Pizza is the best food. **O**
   3) People need food and water to live. **F**
   4) Green shirts look better than blue shirts. **O**
   5) Roses are very pretty. **O**

d. Read this passage with your student.

> *Deer stood and turned around. He saw a fawn looking over the brook. "Little Fawn, why do you look so sad?" asked Deer.*
> *"I am really tired of eating the same food every day. The grass on the other side of the brook is greener," said Fawn.*
> *"My dear little Fawn, take my word for it. The grass is not greener on the other side."*

Ask your student to underline the exact words Fawn said to Deer. When Fawn says the grass on the other side of the brook is greener, he is comparing this grass to the grass on the other side of the brook. Tell your student that when we compare two things, we often add **-er** to the end of the describing word.
Ex: This tree is *taller* than that tree.

e. Help your student make up a comparing sentence for the pictures using **-er.**
Read the following examples to your student.
1) Ex: The spotted box is bigger than the striped box.

striped box   spotted box

2) Ex: The white circle is fatter than the gray circle.

◯ ◯

3) Ex: Bill is smaller than Joe.

Joe   Bill

f. How Do You Spell That Word?

Give your student a piece of paper. You will dictate the spelling words to him guiding him through the process by helping him with spelling rules. Read the following sections that your student needs to correctly spell the words.

Sometimes, when we hear a /j/ sound following a short vowel sound at the end of a word, it is spelled with **dg**. *These words are followed by a silent* **e**.
1) *fudge*   2) *bridge*

Sometimes, when we hear a /ch/ sound at the end of a word, it is spelled **tch**.
3) *match*   4) *watch*

g. Reread the passage in **2d** with your student. Ask him to circle the words that have **oo** in the middle of the word. **stood, looking, brook, look, food**

Tell your student that **oo** makes two different sounds: /oo/ as in *too* and /oo/ as in *look*.

Teacher's Note: These two oo sounds are very similar.

Find page 167 in the *Student Activity Book* and ask your student to cut out the word boxes for **2g**. Put the **oo** sound cards next to each other. Read the word cards with your student and help him decide which group they go in by sound. After the student has placed the cards in groups, check them, and ask him to glue them on paper.
/oo/ in *too* - **school, soon, food, spool, tool, moon, mood, cool**
/oo/ in *look* - **book, took, stood, good, cook, look, wood, foot**

h. Find page 163 in the *Student Activity Book* and ask your student to complete it.

Day 3

a. Review the story for this week.

b. Read this passage with your student.

> *"Yes, Rabbit, but I am really tired of eating the same food every day."*
> *"But Deer, this grass is green, cool, and yummy. I must be on my way. Have a good day, Deer," said Rabbit.*

Ask your student how Rabbit describes the grass. Underline these describing words. **green, cool, yummy** Show your student how these words are written in the passage, and point out the commas. When we have two or more describing words, we separate them with commas and put the word. Ask your student to circle the commas.

Teacher's Note: Some grammar books teach this skill omitting the last comma before the word *and*. Both ways are correct.

Ask your student to put commas in the correct place.
Ex: That tree is big, green, and full.

1) **The box is green, big, and square.**
2) **The girl's hair is long, shiny, and curly.**
3) **This book is funny, exciting, and interesting.**
4) **My puppy is cute, little, and friendly.**

c. Context Words: *special   really   morning*

1) The evening is so nice, but I like the *morning* better.
2) Thank you for the *special* lunch.
3) I am glad you came to see me. I am *really* glad.

 d. Ask your student to find a picture in a magazine or catalog to glue on a piece of paper. Then ask him to write a sentence using with three describing words. Ask him to do one or two of these picture/sentence sheets.

e. Ask your student to complete the Spelling Words Puzzle.

1) fudge   **2) match**   **3) bridge**   **4) watch**

f. Find page 164 in the *Student Activity Book* and ask him to trace the sentence on the top of the page.

Day 4

a. Review the Word List below for "The Grass on the Other Side."

good   *brook*   *took*   *stood*   *noon*   *food*
soon   *cool*   *mood*   *bounded*   *special*   *really*

b. Read this poem with your student.

Hey, Diddle, Diddle

Hey, diddle, diddle,
The cat and the fiddle,
The cow jumped over the moon.
The little dog laughed
To see such sport,
And the dish ran away with the spoon.

Discuss real and make-believe stories, and ask your student to decide if this rhyme
tells about something real or make-believe. Why or why not? If you have a poetry
book, read several poems to or with your student and discuss the real and make-
believe parts of them.

c. Talk with your student about the picture on page 165 of the *Student Activity Book*.
Discuss a story idea about this picture that would be a real story. Suggestion: Two
children walked down the path and saw a rabbit. They stood still and watched him.

Discuss a story idea that would be make-believe. Suggestion: The rabbit tipped his
hat and said to the children, "Come with me, and I'll show you the forest."

Ask your student to write or dictate two to three sentences that would be a real story
and two to three sentences that would be make-believe. Have the student write the real
story on page 165 of the *Student Activity Book* and the make-believe story on page 166
of the *Student Activity Book*.

d. Help your student number a piece of paper 1 - 4. Dictate the spelling words to your student. If he has any difficulty at all, use the same process used in **2f**.

e. Find page 164 in the *Student Activity Book* and ask your student to copy the sentence on the bottom line and color the page. He may take two days to complete this assignment.

Day 5

a. Ask your student to read the story, "The Grass on the Other Side," aloud. Celebrate his success and add to his Reading Chart.

b. Find page 167 in the *Student Activity Book*. Remind your student how to put words in alphabetical order. Show him by example. Ask him to cut out the big boxes in **5b** by number, then cut out the word boxes in number 1 and put them in alphabetical order. Do the same with boxes 2 - 6.
   1) **blow goat jump road**   4) **big cat dog fix**
   2) **blue green red yellow** 5) **ship work yes zoo**
   3) **cold down hot up**   6) **light moon nice pit**

c. Find page 169 in the *Student Activity Book*. Follow the directions to make a Cool Brook Word Wheel. Turn the wheel and read the words with your student. **wood, food, brook, mood, foot, spool, soon, shook, cool, book**

d. There is a guessing game where the players try to guess a word or the name of something by pantomime. The game is called charades. Play charades with words or names.

   Write the words on index cards or pieces of paper, so the players can choose one. Take turns choosing a word and acting it out. Possible words: heavy, big, fly, loud, corn, yawn, under, first, flew, world, wrong, watch.

e. Optional: Spelling test

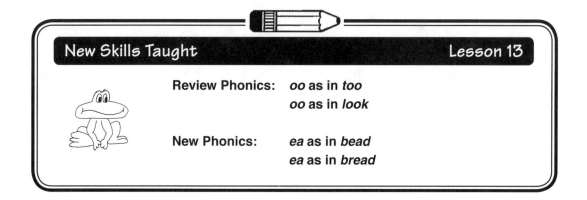

Review Phonics: *oo* as in *too*
                    oo as in *look*

New Phonics: *ea* as in *bead*
                    ea as in *bread*

Day 1

> **Material needed:**
> *Forest Fables*
>
> **props for play**

a. Find the story, "Two Heads are Better than One," in the reader, *Forest Fables*. Read it to or with your student.

b. Discuss the story with your student.

   1) *Tell me the story in your own words.*
   2) *Why did Beaver think Raccoon could not help him?*
   3) *Raccoon did have talents that would help Beaver. What were these talents?* **He knew how to find information in books and he wanted to help Beaver.**
   4) *Beaver said, "Two heads are better than one." What does Beaver mean?* **Two people working on a problem is better than just one because people have different talents.**
   5) *Do you think this is true? Why or why not?*

c. Read this passage with your student.

> *Beaver drew a plan in the mud. He looked at it. He shook his head. It did not look like it would work. Raccoon came by. "You look sad, Beaver. Can I help you?"*

There are two types of sentences in this passage. One is a telling sentence that ends with a period: *Beaver drew a plan in the mud.*

Ask your student to read the other type of sentence to you. **Can I help you?** That is an asking sentence, so it ends with a question mark (**?**).

Asking sentences often begin with one of these words: who, what, when, where, why, or how. Ask your student to read each of the sentences and put a period (.) or a question mark (**?**) at the end of each sentence.

1) **When is the game?**   5) **My name is Bill.**
2) **I like to play baseball.**   6) **The dog is black and white.**
3) **Where is your house?**   7) **How do you make cookies?**
4) **What time is it?**   8) **She is my friend.**

d. Ask your student to look at the picture and read the sentences. Put an X beside the sentence that best describes the picture.

___1) It was noon by the time they got to the brook.
X 2) She is reading a book.
___3) Soon we will read the story.
___4) The wood house shook in the wind.

e. Ask your student to copy the spelling words for this week. Read them to or with your student: *stood   stool   shook   mood.*

Day 2

a. Review the story for this week with your student.

b. Talk to your student about the emotions in this story.

1) *Beaver is having a hard time with his project. How do you think he feels before Raccoon comes by?* **frustrated, upset, confused**
2) *How does Beaver feel when Raccoon is offering his help?* **mad**
3) *How does Beaver feel at the end of the story?* **happy**
4) *Retell the story as if you are Beaver and express his emotion as you tell it.*
Possible answers: I was making plans for a new dam. It was not going well. I had some problems I could not figure out. Raccoon came by to help, but I foolishly told him I did not need help, etc.

c. Ask your student to read the word lists and draw lines to match the words and make compound words.

some — side
be — one
pea — man
mail — set
sun — nut

d. How Do You Spell That Word?

Give your student a piece of paper. You will dictate the spelling words to him guiding him through the process by helping him with spelling rules. Read the following sections that your student needs to correctly spell the words.

*We have learned that the letters **oo** make two different sounds: /oo/ in too and /ŏŏ/ in cook.*
Ask your student to say the words aloud as he writes them.
1) stood   2) stool   3) shook   4) mood

e. Read this passage with your student.

Beaver already had a dam on the river. He wanted one on the bank instead of over a tree. A dam on the edge of the steep bank would be harder to make.

Ask your student to find two words that have the vowel combination **ea** and circle them. **already instead** We have learned that **ea** usually says /ē/ as in *bead*, but sometimes it says /ĕ/ as in *head*. Ask your student to read these /ĕ/ words with you: *bread   head   read (/rĕd/) tread   instead   ready   lead (/lĕd/).*

Teacher's Note: The pronunciation of the words *read* and *lead* will be further discussed in 3c.

Find page 177 in the *Student Activity Book*. Ask your student to cut out the word boxes for **2e** and put the Sound Cards in a row. Then read each word card with your student and ask him to put it below the correct Sound Card. Ask him to read each row of words to you.
ea /ē/ - beak meat beach teach team clean seat heat
ea /ĕ/ - ready spread dead bread tread

f. Find page 179 in the *Student Activity Book* and ask your student to complete it.

Day 3

a. Review the story for this week with your student.

b. Act out the story, "Two Heads are Better than One," with your student. Switch parts, so your student can play both characters. Use props if possible.

c. Reread the list of words from **2e** to your student: *bread head read tread instead ready lead.*

There are two words in this list that can be said two different ways. Show your student the words *read* and *lead*. Tell him that the **ea** in these two words can say /ē/ or /ĕ/.

Ask him to read each word with the /ĕ/ sound and then with the /ē/ sound. These words have different meanings when they have different sounds. These words are called homonyms. My pencil is made out of *lead*. The Captain will *lead* his men. Other homonyms sound the same but are spelled differently. I *see* the moon. The boat is on the *sea*.

Teacher's Note: Some grammar books refer to words like *lead* and *lead* as homographs; they also refer to words like *see* and *sea* as homophones.

Find page 177 in the *Student Activity Book*. Tell your student to cut out the word cards for **3c**. Read the words to or with your student. Ask him to match the homonyms. **two-to, sun-son, knew-new, won-one, eight-ate, bee-be**

d. Context Words: *above*
The bridge is *above* the river.

e. Ask your student to complete the Spelling Words Puzzle.
1) shook   2) stood   3) mood   4) stool

f. Find page 180 in the *Student Activity Book* and ask him to trace the sentence on the top of the page.

Day 4

a. Review the Word List below for "Two Heads are Better than One."

already	*instead*	*head*	*read*
raccoon	*sure*	*above*	*maybe*

b. Ask your student to write the contraction for these words. Give him any help he needs to be successful with the activity. Ex: can not - can't
1) did not - **didn't**   2) she is - **she's**   3) they are - **they're**
4) we will - **we'll**   5) I am - **I'm**   6) it is - **it's**

c. Talk to your student about the people and objects in the picture. He is going to make up a story about this picture. Use any questions that are helpful.

   1) *What do you see the boy doing in the picture? What is the mother doing?*
   2) *What do you think happened just before this picture? What happened just after the picture?*
   3) *How is the boy feeling in the picture? How is the mom feeling?*

Ask your student to tell you a story about the picture. He can name the people and tell what happened before or after the picture. After the discussion, ask him to write or dictate three to four sentences about the picture. Suggest using different types of sentences in the story: declarative, interrogative, and exclamatory. He may want to color the picture.

d. Help your student number a piece of paper 1 - 4. Dictate the spelling words to your student. If he has any difficulty at all, use the same process used in **2d**.

e. Find page 180 in the *Student Activity Book* and ask your student to copy the sentence on the bottom line and color the page. He may take two days to complete this assignment.

Day 5

a. Ask your student to read the story, "Two Heads are Better than One," aloud. Celebrate his success and add to his Reading Chart.

b. Ask your student to tell you the antonyms, or opposites, of these words.

   1) *wide* - **narrow**   2) *empty* - **full**   3) *far* - **near**

Find page 177 in the *Student Activity Book* and ask your student to cut out the word boxes for **5b**. Then tell him to match the words that are opposites. Ex: high - low

1) **in - out**	2) **up - down**	3) **hot - cold**
4) **late - early**	5) **big - little**	6) **off - on**

Optional: Ask him to draw pictures to go with each opposite pair.

 c. Using butcher paper, ask your student to lay flat on the paper and trace around him. You may use brown paper bags, cutting and taping them together to make a large enough sheet. Ask your student to draw clothes on the body shape you traced. Ask him to tell you the name of each clothing part, as you label it, or he may label it himself. Encourage your student to be as complete as possible.

Ask him to put his name on the bottom of the sheet. You may want to hang up the picture he has drawn of himself. Using a tape measure, help your student measure his picture and write his height on it.

d. Optional: Spelling test

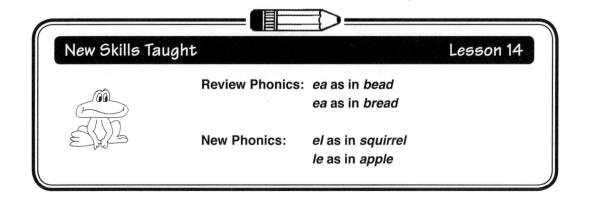

Review Phonics: *ea* as in *bead*
ea as in *bread*

New Phonics: *el* as in *squirrel*
le as in *apple*

Day 1

Materials needed:
Forest Fables

Ox-Cart Man by Donald Hall

pictures from magazines, catalogs or newspapers

a. Find the story, "Actions Speak Louder than Words," in the reader, *Forest Fables*. Read it to or with your student.

b. Discuss the story with your student.

   1) *Tell me the story in your own words.* **Self-explanatory**
   2) *Why did Raccoon think that Squirrel wanted to help him move the big branches?* **Squirrel said he would.** *Why didn't he help Raccoon?* **He wanted to do other things first.**
   3) *Why did Raccoon make hot chocolate?* **He knew squirrel liked it.**
   4) *How was Rabbit different from Squirrel? Tell me more about that.* **Rabbit did what he said he would do.**
   5) *"Actions speak louder than words." What does this mean?* **The things we do mean more than the things we say.**

c. Read this passage to or with your student.

   Raccoon was working in his yard. Lots of branches, twigs, and other dead wood were left after the storm. He got his shovel and put them in a circle. There were three big branches to carry to the pile. They were very heavy. He went to Squirrel to ask for help.

Ask your student how many twigs were on the ground in Raccoon's yard. **two or more** How do we know there was more than one twig on the ground? **The s at the end of the word tells us.**

Ask him to find the word *branches* and circle it. Ask your student to look at the word, *branch*. Ask him what letters are added to show more than one branch. **es**

If you say *twigs* and *branches*, you can hear a difference in the plural **s** sound. Since it sounds differently, it is spelled differently. Here's the rule:

To make a naming word mean more than one (plural), just add **s**. If a naming word ends in **ch**, **sh**, **s**, or **x**, add **es**.

Read these words with your student. Ask him to make them plural and copy them into the correct blank. *bunch bush ax kiss*

1) There are two chopping **axes** in the barn.
2) Dad gave me five **kisses** when he got home from work.
3) Mom got three **bunches** of grapes for us.
4) There are four flower **bushes** in our front yard.

d. Reread the passage with your student. There are two words that have **ea** in the middle of them. Ask your student to circle the words. **dead heavy** Read these words with your student, and remind him that **ea** usually says /ē/, but it can also say /ĕ/ as in *head*.

Ask your student to read each sentence and put an X next to the sentence that best describes the picture.

___1) Sally put the plate on her head.
___2) The window is clear.
_X_3) Mom said dinner would be ready soon.
___4) We are having bread for dinner.
___5) It is a year until my next birthday.

Write a sentence about this picture. Use a proper noun in your sentence.

e. Ask your student to copy the spelling words for this week. Read them to or with your student: *were looking worked head*.

Day 2

a. Review the story for this week with your student.

b. Today, we will compare Rabbit and Squirrel. Talk to your student about each of these characters. How are they alike and how are they different? Find *Student Activity Book* page 191 and ask your student to cut out the pictures of Rabbit and Squirrel and the Phrase Boxes for **2b**. Read the phrases with your student and help him decide if it goes best with Rabbit or Squirrel. Do this with all the phrases. Glue it all on paper.

knows Raccoon needs help
says he will help Raccoon
does not keep Raccoon waiting
helps Raccoon
drinks hot chocolate

knows Raccoon needs help
says he will help Raccoon
keeps Raccoon waiting for help
does not help Raccoon
drinks hot chocolate

c. Read this passage with or to your student.

>   *Raccoon sat in the yard. He felt terrible. "I do not want to quarrel with Squirrel. He said that he would help."*
>   *Rabbit rode his bicycle down the road. He was eating an apple. "Raccoon, you look sad. Would you like some bubble gum?"*

Ask your student to read the first sentence aloud. Remind him that a sentence is made up of two parts:
1) the subject, or who or what the sentence is about
2) the predicate, the part that tells something about the subject

Ask your student to underline the part of the first sentence that tells who or what the sentence is about. **Raccoon**

Ask him to underline with two lines, the part of the sentence that tells what Raccoon is doing in the sentence. <u>sat in the yard</u> Ask him to do the same with the fifth and sixth sentences. Remind him that a pronoun, such as *he*, can be the subject.

fifth sentence - **Rabbit <u>rode his bicycle down the road</u>.**

sixth sentence - **He <u>was eating an apple</u>.**

d. How Do You Spell That Word?

Give your student a piece of paper. You will dictate the spelling words to him guiding him through the process.
1) *were - This is a common word.* Tell him how to spell it if needed.
2) *worked - Words that begin the /wer/ sound are spelled **wor**.*
   *The /d/ sound added to the end of a word is spelled -**ed**.*
3) *head - The /ĕ/ sound in the middle of a word can be spelled **ea**.*
4) *looking - The /o͝o/ sound in the middle of a word can be spelled **oo**.*
   *The sound /ing/ is spelled -**ing**.*

e. Reread the literature passage with your student. There are several words that end with **el** or **le**. Ask your student to circle all these words. **terrible, quarrel, squirrel, bicycle, apple, bubble** Read them to him and ask him what sound the **el** and **le** make in the word. **the /l/ sound** Tell him that words that end in **le, el**, or **al** have the /l/ sound. Ask him to look through the whole story and find any words that end with **el** or **le**. Say these words aloud with your student.
Possible answers: shovel circle pile Squirrel travel kettle table terrible quarrel bicycle apple bubble simple

f. Find page 187 in the *Student Activity Book* and ask your student to complete it.

Day 3

a. Review the story for this week with your student.

b. Reread the literature passage from **2c** with your student. Remind him that a noun is a naming word. There are some little words that often come before a naming word that tell us that a naming word is coming. The words *a, an,* and *the* are called articles.

Look for the word *yard* in the literature passage. *Yard* is a naming word, or noun. Underline the little word that comes before the word *yard*. **<u>the</u> yard**

Look for the word *apple* in the literature passage. Underline the little word that comes before the word *apple*. **<u>an</u> apple**

We see in our sentences *an apple, the road,* and *the yard.* The little words *a, an,* and *the* tell us that a naming word is coming.

Teacher's Note: We will not define them as articles at this point.

Look back at the passage in **1c**. Using a red crayon or pencil, underline the words *a* and *the.* What do they tell us is coming? **a naming word or noun** With a blue crayon, underline the naming word that comes next. **the storm, a circle, the pile**

Ask your student to read these sentences and circle the words *a, an* or *the* and underline the noun that follows.
1) Mom gave me **an apple**.
2) **The dog** likes to run and play.
3) I want to go to **the park**.
4) Where is **an animal** book?
5) We are going to **the store**.
6) Dad wants to take **a picture**.

c. Context Words: *chocolate   move   actions*
   1) The turtle will *move* very slowly.
   2) I like to drink hot *chocolate* on a cold day.
   3) The name of our story is "*Actions* Speak Louder than Words."

Syllable Sense: When a word ends in a **consonant -le**, we divide the word before the consonant that comes before the **le**. Look at *table.* When we divide it before the **b**, the **a** says /ā/: ta / ble.

Teacher's Note: ck words are exceptions. Words like *chuckle, tickle, tackle, buckle, knuckle* are divided before le.

 d. On a piece of blank paper ask your student to write his name in BIG letters. Then write it as small as possible. Then write it in many different colors.

e. Ask your student to complete the Spelling Words Puzzle.
   1) head   2) were   3) looking   4) worked

f. Find page 188 in the *Student Activity Book* and ask him to trace the sentence on the top of the page.

Day 4

4. a. Review the Word List below for "Actions Speak Louder Than Words."

   Squirrel   *travel*   *quarrel*   *towel*   *kettle*   *apple*
   table   *bubble*   *terrible*   *simple*   *final*   *chocolate*

   b. Read the story, *Ox-Cart Man* by Donald Hall, to your student. Discuss the events of the story with him.

   Find page 185 in the *Student Activity Book*. There is a section for each season. Using the book, *Ox-Cart Man*, ask your student to find pictures, words, and phrases that describe each season. Ask him to write or dictate words in a list on each season's section.

   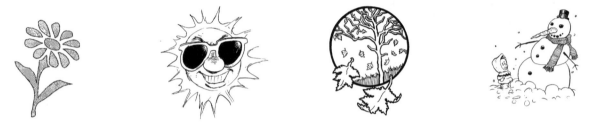

   c. Reread the passage in **1c** with your student. In the fourth sentence is the naming word *branches*. Ask your student to find the two words that describe *branches*. **three, big** Describing words tell us about naming words. These words can be numbers, colors, sizes, and other types of describing words.

   Read this sentence with your student: *There is a tree in my yard*.

   Ask your student how he would illustrate this sentence. It is hard to know how to draw the tree.

   Read this sentence with your student: *The big oak tree shades a corner of my yard*.

   On a separate piece of paper, ask your student to copy this sentence on the bottom of his sheet. Ask him to illustrate this sentence. Ask him if he knows the kind of picture to draw and why.

   Talk to your student about the words that could be added to the sentence to describe the tree. Ask him to add these words and illustrate the sentence. **Possible answers: tall, full, green, bushy**

   d. Help your student number a piece of paper 1 - 4. Dictate the spelling words to your student. If he has any difficulty at all, use the same process used in **2d**.

   e. Find page 188 in the *Student Activity Book* and ask your student to copy the sentence on the bottom line and color the page. He may take two days to complete this assignment.

Day 5

5. a. Ask your student to read the story, "Actions Speak Louder than Words," aloud. Celebrate his success and add to his Reading Chart.

   b. Find a picture in a magazine, catalog, or newspaper and cut it out. Glue it on a piece of paper. Ask your student to write or dictate two describing sentences about the picture.

 c. Find the pictures of the four trees on page 189 in the *Student Activity Book*. Cut out the four squares, and ask your student to decorate each tree for each season. Fold the tab under on each section and glue the tabs of each tree on a piece of construction paper. Ask your student to write two to three describing words in front of each tree.

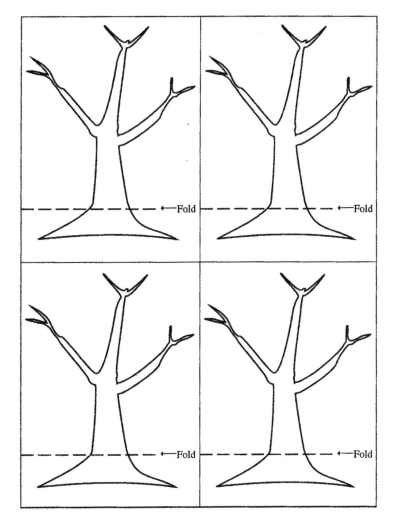

   d. Optional: Spelling test

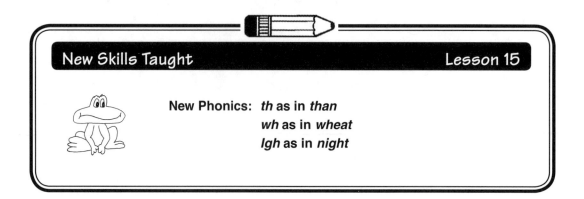

New Phonics: *th* as in *than*

wh as in *wheat*

Igh as in *night*

Materials needed:
Forest Fables

craft materials

✎ **Teacher's Note:**
If your student questions
the one-word sentence,
tell him it is acceptable.

Day 1

a. Find the story, "Two Wrongs Do Not Make a Right," in the reader, *Forest Fables*. Read it to or with your student.

b. Discuss the story with your student.

1) *Tell me the story in your own words.* **Self-explanatory**
2) *Why did Badger want to destroy Beaver's dam?* **Beaver accidentally broke her house.**
3) *What part did Rabbit play in this story?* **a peacemaker** *Was that an important thing for him to do?*
4) *How would you have felt if you were Badger in the story? If you were Beaver? If you were Rabbit?* **Answers will vary.**
5) *Did you like the ending of the story? Why or why not?* **Allow for discussion.**

c. Read this passage to or with your student.

"Upset!" yelled Badger. "I am more than upset. How would you feel if your house were broken by a tree?"

There are three different types of sentences in this passage. Ask your student to find the three different end marks and circle each one. (**!** . **?**) Remind him that we use an exclamation mark when the sentence shows strong emotion. Ask him to read the first sentence as Badger would say it.

Ask your student to read each sentence and add the correct end mark.

1) She is late for the show**.**
2) Will you go with me to the store**?**
3) Wow, look at this**!**
4) He likes tuna**.**
5) Should I call Dad now**?**

d. In the passage there is a word that begins with **th**. Ask your student to find it and circle it. **than** The **t** and **h** in this word work together to make one sound. What is that sound? **/th/**

Look at the word *wheat*. The **w** and **h** work together to make one sound. What is that sound? **/w/**

Read the words in the Phonics Word Box with your student: *this   that   white   while   wheel*.

Ask your student to look at the picture, read the sentences and put an X next to the sentence that best describes the picture.

_X_ 1) My white bear is in the toy box.

___ 2) There is a wheel on my car.

___ 3) I saw this and that at the zoo.

___ 4) I will eat dinner in a short while.

Write a sentence about the picture using at least two naming words, or nouns.

e. Ask your student to copy the spelling words for this week. Read them to or with your student: *took   final   table   wrong*.

Day 2

2. a. Review the story for this week with your student.

b. At the end of our story Badger says that she can see now that two wrongs do not make a right. Ask your student what he thinks that means. Can he think of anytime when that proverb may be helpful to him or someone he knows?

c. Find page 203 in the *Student Activity Book*. Ask your student to cut out each picture for **2c** and put them in the correct order of the story. After you have checked them, glue the pictures onto paper and have your student write or dictate one sentence under each picture telling what is happening in the picture.

d. We have already talked about putting words in alphabetical order using the first letter in the word. Review that if needed. Find page 203 in the *Student Activity Book*. Ask your student to cut out the word cards: *goat   gate   grape* for **2d**. Ask him how he thinks he can put those words in alphabetical order.

When the first letter is the same in a list of words, we use the second letter to put them in alphabetical order. Ask him to put the words in ABC order: **gate   goat   grape**.

On page 203 in the *Student Activity Book*, there are four bigger boxes for your student to cut out for **2d**. In box 1 there are four small word cards. Ask him to cut those out and put them in ABC order.

1) **ran rest rim rug**

Ask him to do the same with boxes 2, 3 and 4.

2) **get glad goat grab**
3) **sack sit star sun**
4) **bat bed bike bud**

e. How Do You Spell That Word?

Give your student a piece of paper. You will dictate the spelling words to him guiding him through the process.

1) *took - The /oo/ sound is sometimes spelled **oo**.*
2) *final - The /l/ sound is usually spelled **le**, **el**, or **al**.*
3) *table - If needed, use the rule in 2.*
4) *wrong - At the beginning of a word, the /r/ sound can be spelled **wr**.*

f. Read to or with your student the proverb from our story this week: *Two wrongs do not make a right*. Ask your student to find the word *right* and circle it. What sounds does your student hear in this word? /r/, /ī/, /t/ Ask him if he can think of a rule about the letters and the sounds in *right*. **The igh says /ī/; gh is silent.** Ask him to read these words aloud remembering this rule: *night might fight sigh sight right*

Ask your student to read the words in the Phonics Word Box and choose the best word to complete the sentences: *night might fight sigh sight right*

Ask him to copy the correct word to complete these sentences.
1) Should I turn left or **right**?
2) He used all his **might** to lift that box.
3) The owl hoots at **night**.

g. Find page 201 in the *Student Activity Book* and ask your student to complete it.

Day 3

  a. Review the story for this week with your student.

  b. A summary is a short version of a story. Ask your student to read this summary of our story this week.

> *Badger is going to smash Beaver's house because she is angry about her house being broken by Beaver's old tree. Rabbit talks to Badger about her choices. Badger decides not to smash the house. Everyone will help Badger build a new house.*

Ask your student to circle the word that tells whose house Badger is going to smash.
Beaver's
Ask him to circle the word that tells whose old tree broke Badger's house.
Beaver's
Ask your student what was added to the word *Beaver* to show that the house and tree belonged to him. **apostrophe and s ('s)**

Remind your student that there is a special pronoun that shows the house belongs to Beaver. Ask him to read this sentence, tell you the possessive pronoun, and underline it. *Badger was going to smash his house.* **his**

Ask your student to read these possessive pronouns and copy them in the correct blanks: *his her their*.

  1) Badger had **her** house broken.
  2) Rabbit used **his** head to solve the problem.
  3) Rabbit and Beaver had a plan, and Badger liked **their** plan.
  4) Badger will like **her** new house.

  c. Context Words: *purpose build together*.

  1) Rabbit and Beaver will help Badger *build* her new house.
  2) What is the *purpose* of the story?
  3) Let's work on this job *together*.

Syllable Sense: Remind your student that if the syllable of a word ends with a vowel, the vowel will usually say its long sound. Ex: **be / low**

Ask him to divide the word *apart*. **a/part**

d. Ask your student to fold a piece of blank paper in half. Fold it in half the other way. Open it up and he will have four sections.

   In each section, ask him to choose a word from "Two Wrongs Do Not Make a Right," write it and illustrate the word. He may copy the word from the reader.

e. Ask your student to complete the Spelling Words Puzzle.
   1) **final**   2) **took**   3) **wrong**   4) **table**

   The word in the box is foot.

f. Find page 202 in the *Student Activity Book* and ask him to trace the sentence on the top of the page.

Day 4

a. Review the Word List below for "Two Wrongs Do Not Make a Right."

right	*night*	*sighed*	*fight*	*might*
mumbled	*normal*	*purpose*	*build*	*together*

b. Look through the reader, *Forest Fables,* with your student. Talk about the characters, stories, and setting. Discuss it with your student.

   1) *Which characters do you like? Why?*
   2) *Which stories did you like? Why?*
   3) *What do you like about the pictures?*
   4) Show your student the title page and read the title, author, illustrator, and publisher. *Do you know what the author did for this book?* **She wrote the book**. *What did the illustrator do for this book?* **She drew the pictures**. *What did the publisher do for this book?* **He had the book printed and sent it to the stores so we could buy it**.
   5) Show your student the copyright page and table of contents. *The copyright page tells you more about the book and the publisher. It also tells us we cannot copy this book and sell or give it someone. The table of contents tell us on what page each story begins.*

c. Find pages 205 in the *Student Activity Book*. There are several pictures of the characters and objects from the reader, *Forest Fables,* for **4c**. Discuss these Forest Project ideas with your student and ask him to choose a Forest Project to work on today and tomorrow.

    1) Color and cut out pictures. Use a shoe box and create a 3-D scene, or diorama, of the farm. Your student may write or dictate a summary of a few stories from the reader or make up his own.

    2) Color and cut out pictures. Create a sentence about six of the pictures. Glue the pictures on the top of a paper and write the sentence under each picture.

    3) Create a new story about our farm friends. Color and cut out the pictures. Make a book by stapling several pages together. Write the story in the book, and glue the pictures in as desired.

d. Help your student number a piece of paper 1 - 4. Dictate the spelling words to your student. If he has any difficulty at all, use the same process used in **2e**.

e. Find page 202 in the *Student Activity Book* and ask your student to copy the sentence on the bottom line and color the page. He may take two days to complete this assignment.

Day 5

a. Ask your student to read the story, "Two Wrongs Do Not Make a Right," aloud. Celebrate his success and add to his Reading Chart. He has now completed *Forest Fables*. Have your student glue this reading cover on his Reading Chart.

b. Continue work on the Forest Project.

c. Prepare to present it to a group.

d. Optional: Spelling test

e. Complete *Assessment 3* with your student.

Assessment 3
(Lessons 11 - 15)

This is the oral part of *Assessment 3*.

1. *Contractions are a shortened way of joining two words together with an apostrophe. For example,* can't *is a contraction for* can not. *Tell me the contraction for these words.*

   a. *we will* **we'll**
   b. *did not* **didn't**
   c. *it is* **it's**
   d. *she is* **she's**
   e. *they are* **they're**
   f. *I am* **I'm**

2. *Stories can be real or make-believe. Tell me if these sentences are real or make-believe, and why.*

   a. *The lazy lion yawned as he woke up from his nap. He looked at the clock. He was hungry.* **Make-believe, lions do not have clocks.**
   b. *The lion woke up from his nap. He gazed across the plains. Food was scarce during the drought.* **Real, these are all things real lions do.**

3. *Every sentence has two parts: the subject, who or what the sentence is about; and the predicate, the part that tells something about the subject. Listen to this sentence and tell me the subject, or who or what the sentence is about. Repeat the sentence as necessary.*

   The boys *swam in the lake.*

   What did the subject do? **swam, or swam in the lake**

This is the written part of *Assessment 3*. Ask your student to find pages 198-199 in his *Student Activity Book*, and ask him to complete it as you instruct him.

1. *There are three types of sentences: a telling sentence, an asking sentence, and a sentence that shows strong feeling. Every sentence must have an end mark. Write a period (.), a question mark (?), or an exclamation mark (!) after each sentence.*

   a. Watch out for that step**!**
   b. It is nice to see you**.**
   c. How are you**?**

2. *Add **-ed** and **-ing** to these words.*

   a. jump   **jumped**   **jumping**
   b. bat   **batted**   **batting**
   c. dine   **dined**   **dining**

3. *Put these words in alphabetical order:*

   a. **fence   nice   port   ship   young**
   b. **rat   risk   rock   rope   run**

4. *A, an, and the are special words that tell us a naming word is coming. Circle these words and underline the naming word that follows.*

   a. I saw (an) <u>elephant</u>.
   b. Please give her (a) <u>present</u>.
   c. He ate (the) <u>piece</u> of bread.

5. *Commas are used to separate two or more adjectives. Put commas in these sentences.*

   a. Mom made a tasty, hot meal.
   b. I gave her a big, wet kiss.

6. *Most words make their plural by just adding **s**, as in* one cat *and* two cats. *Words ending in **ch**, **sh**, **s**, and **x** make their plural form by adding **-es**. Add **-es** to these words.*

   a. church - **churches**
   b. tax - **taxes**
   c. dish - **dishes**
   d. glass - **glasses**

7. *Read the sentences. Rewrite the sentences by changing the possessive noun to a possessive pronoun.*

   a. Jack rode *Jack's* bike. **Jack rode his bike.**
   b. Mom and Dad visited *Mom and Dad's* friends. **Mom and Dad visited their friends.**
   c. Sara brought *Sara's* dog. **Sara brought her dog.**

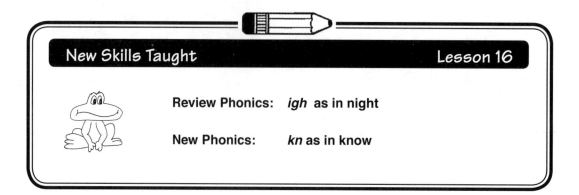

Review Phonics: *igh* as in night

New Phonics: *kn* as in know

Material needed:
In, Out, and About Catfish Pond

Corduroy by Don Freeman

Day 1

a. Find the story, "New Shoes, Yellow Shoes," in the reader, *In, Out, and About Catfish Pond.* Read it to or with your student.

b. Discuss the story with your student.

   1) *In our story, the residents of Catfish Pond have a problem. It seems that Beaver is very excited about his new shoes. What does Beaver do with his new shoes?* **He shows them to everyone and is very loud about it.**

   2) *It is normal to be excited about something new. Have you ever gotten anything new that you were excited about? How did you act? Did you want to tell everyone?*

   3) *Turtle and Muskrat were very honest with Beaver. What effect did it have on Beaver?* **It hurt Beaver's feelings.**

   4) *How did Otter explain his feelings to Beaver? What did Otter say that helped Beaver?* **If Beaver liked his shoes, then they were right for him.**

   5) *Have you ever really liked something that others didn't like? Did they say hurtful things? Tell me about it.*

   6) *Do you think you should always give your opinion?*

c. Read the passage with your student.

   Muskrat and Turtle walked away quickly.

Show your student how to spell the word *quick.* Tell him that the suffix **-ly** is added to the word to describe how Muskrat and Turtle walked. Ask him to circle the word *quickly.*

Ask your student to add **-ly** to these words. Tell him to write the new word, and then read the base word and new word to you.
glad - **gladly,** slow - **slowly,** sad - **sadly,** neat - **neatly.**

d. Look at the title of the reader with your student: *In, Out, and About Catfish Pond.* Remind your student that sometimes two words are joined together to make a new word. These words are called compound words.

Ask him to tell you the compound word in the title of the reader, and to tell you the two words which make up the new word. **catfish -** *cat* **and** *fish* If your student does not know, explain to him that a catfish is a type of fish that has long whiskers like a cat, therefore, the name *catfish.*

e. Read the passage with your student.

> *"I love my new, yellow shoes!"*

Ask your student what kind of shoes Beaver had. Underline these describing words. **new, yellow** When two or more describing words come before a noun, you separate the describing words with a comma. Circle the comma in the passage.

Add commas in these sentences.

1) Turtle put her head in her shiny**,** hard shell.
2) Otter wore his old**,** brown hat.
3) Muskrat showed his sharp**,** clean teeth.

 f. Ask your student if he remembers the sound **igh** makes as in the word *night.* **long /ī/ sound** Read the words in the Phonics Word Box with your student: *night   right   might   sigh.*

Ask your student to complete the sentences using one of the **igh** words.
1) I turned left and then **right**.
2) The owl howled in the **night**.
3) They heard the boy give a **sigh** at the end of the poem.
4) I ran with all my **might**.

0

g. Using sturdy paper, manila drawing paper, or light colored construction paper, ask your student to draw Beaver's new shoes. Prepare your student to do this by going through the story again and finding the describing words, or adjectives, that tell about Beaver's shoes. Make a list of these words as you and your student find them.

Ask him to draw the shoes and make up phrases describing the shoes using words from the list, such as *new shoes*, or *big, yellow shoes*. You or your student may write these descriptive phrases on the back of the picture, or below it. Point out to your student that we separate two describing words with a comma. Ex: big, yellow shoes

h. Ask your student to copy the spelling words for this week. Read them to or with your student: *high   right   catfish   though*.

Day 2

a. Review the story, "New Shoes, Yellow Shoes," from the reader, *In, Out, and About Catfish Pond* with your student.

b. Using the new words from **1c**, choose the best word to complete these sentences.

1) I did my job **gladly**.   2) I wrote my name **neatly**.
3) I lost my new toy and walked home **sadly**.   4) The turtle walked **slowly**.

c. Let's review how to add the suffix **-ing** to a word. Ask your student to add **-ing** to the word *fish*. **fishing** *Just add the suffix -ing.*

Ask him how to add **-ing** to the word *stop*. **stopping - double the last consonant and add -ing**

Remember, if a word ends with a short vowel and a consonant, double the last consonant before adding **-ing**. Tell your student to first look at each word and decide if he just adds **-ing**, or if he needs to double the last consonant before adding **-ing**. Write the new words under the correct column.

<u>Just add -ing, as in *fishing*</u>	<u>Double the last consonant, as in *stopping*</u>
jumping	**hitting**
washing	**sitting**
standing	**running**

d. How Do You Spell That Word?

Give your student a piece of paper and a pencil. Dictate the spelling words to your student, guiding him through the process and helping him learn spelling rules.

1) *high* - *Some words spell the* /ī/ *sound with* **igh**.
2) *right* - same as 1.
3) *catfish*
4) *though*

e. Read this sentence with your student: *Sam hurt his knee.*

Tell your student that the word *knee* has a silent letter. Ask him to tell you the silent letter and cross it out. Several words begin with **kn** and always says /**n**/, but words do not end in **kn**. Read the words in the Phonics Word Box with your student, or ask your student to read them to you: *knot   knight   knit   knew knock   knife*.

Day 3

a. Review the story, "New Shoes, Yellow Shoes."

b. Read the passage with your student.

> *Otter looked at the shoes on Beaver's feet. The shoes were too big. The shoes were too bright.*

Ask your student how big were Beaver's shoes. **too big** How bright were his shoes? **too bright** The word *too* in these sentences mean *very*, as in very big and very bright.

Do you know another word that sounds the same as *too*, but has a different meaning? **two, to** Your student will probably say *two*, but may miss *to*. That is acceptable at this time.

Write the word *two* for your student. Tell him that the number word *two* sounds the same as *too*, but has a different meaning and a different spelling.

Write the word *to* for your student. Tell your student that this word is used often, as in "Give this to the boy," or "I will go to the store." Tell him that the word *to* sounds the same as *too* and *two*, but has a different meaning and a different spelling. *Too, two,* and *to* are called homonyms.

Complete the sentences with the correct word.

1) It was **too** cold to play outside.
2) Come **to** dinner.
3) My little sister is **two** years old.

c. Context Words: *shoes   walked.*

1) The zoo was big. We *walked* all day.
2) Beaver was happy about his new *shoes*.

d. Ask your student to complete the Spelling Words Puzzle.
   1) **though**   3) **catfish**
   2) **right**   4) **high**

e. Find page 212 in the *Student Activity Book* and ask your student to trace the sentence on the top.

Day 4

a. Review the Word List below for "New Shoes, Yellow Shoes."
   shoes   walked   Turtle   Otter   quickly   Catfish

b. Read the book, *Corduroy*, by Don Freeman to your student, or he may read it to you.

c. Talk to your student about the book. You may use these questions to help you in your discussion.

   1) *Tell me the story in your own words.* **Self-explanatory**
   2) *Home is a place that is cozy and loving, and a friend is someone who accepts you as you are. What are some of the important things about your family and friends?* **Answers will vary.**
   3) *Where was "home" for Corduroy — on the toy shelf, upstairs in the store, or Lisa's room?* **Lisa's room**

d. Today, review how to add the suffix **-ed** to a word. Read the passage with your student.

   "How do you like my new shoes?" he asked.

Review with your student that for most words, you just add **-ed,** as in the word *asked* used in the passage.

Now, read this passage with your student.

"Why did you say you liked them, Otter?"

Review with your student that if a word ends with a silent **e**, he must first drop the **e** and then add **-ed**, as in the word *liked* used in the passage.

e. Ask your student to add **-ed** to these words: play   bake   shout   clean   paste   rake.

Tell your student to first look at the word and decide if he should just add **-ed**, or if the word ends with a silent **e**, drop the **e** and add **-ed**.

Tell him to write the new words under the correct column. Then ask him to read the base word and the new word to you.

Just add -ed	**Drop the e and add -ed**
played	baked
shouted	pasted
cleaned	raked

f. Ask your student to draw a picture of Corduroy or his favorite bear.

g. Help your student number a piece of paper 1 - 4. Dictate the spelling words to your student. If he has any difficulty at all, use the same process used in **2d**.

h. Find page 212 in the *Student Activity Book* and ask your student to copy the sentence on the bottom line and color the page. He may take two days to complete this assignment.

Day 5

a. Ask your student to read "New Shoes, Yellow Shoes" aloud.

b. Read the passage with your student.

Beaver walked down the path to Catfish Pond. "New shoes! Yellow shoes!" he sang. "I love my new, yellow shoes!"

Ask your student why he thinks a period is at the end of the first sentence. **It is a telling sentence.** Ask your student why he thinks an exclamation mark (**!**) is used at the end of the other sentences. **It shows that the sentence is telling something exciting.**

Read this passage with your student.

"How do you like my new shoes?"

Ask your student why he thinks a question mark **(?)** is used at the end of this sentence. **It is an asking sentence.**

c. Syllable Sense: Remind your student that a word with double consonants in the middle of a word is divided between the double consonants. Ex: Ot/ter

d. Optional: Spelling test

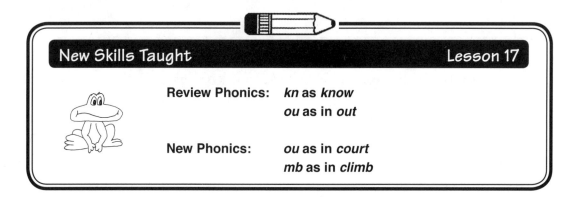

Day 1

Materials needed:
*In, Out, and About
Catfish Pond*

a. Find the story, "Tales About Tails," in the reader, *In, Out, and About Catfish Pond*. Read it to or with your student.

b. Talk to your student about the story. You may use these questions to help you in your discussion.
1) *Beaver and Muskrat got involved in comparing their tails which they both liked very much. What did this comparison lead to?* **Each one thought his tail was better.**
2) *Beaver and Muskrat started telling what they could do with their tails. What did they say they could do?* **They said they could catch fish.**
3) *Beaver and Muskrat were "telling tales."* Explain to your student what "telling tales" means using an incident from your own life. Tell him what happened and the result of telling a tale.
4) *As Beaver and Muskrat tried to be better than each other, they exaggerated more and more.* Read Colossians 3:9 and talk with your student about lying and its consequences. *What did Beaver and Muskrat do at the end of the story that was right?* **They told the truth.**
5) *Have you ever told a lie? Tell me about it. What was the result of telling a lie?*

c. Tell your student that a fact is something that is true and can be proven. An opinion is what someone thinks about something. For example, a fact in the story is that both Muskrat and Beaver had tails. They had different opinions. What was Muskrat's opinion of his tail? **It was the best tail.** What was Beaver's opinion of his tail? **It was the best tail.**

d. Ask your student if he remembers the sound **kn** makes in the word *knee*. **/n/ sound** Read these words with your student: *knot knit knock knife*.

Complete the sentences using one of the **kn** words.
1) Ted will tie a **knot** in the rope.
2) Mom cuts the cake with a **knife**.
3) I heard a **knock** at the door.
4) Grandma will **knit** some socks.

e. Ask your student to copy the spelling words for this week. Read them to or with your student: *knot know knit knife*.

Day 2

a. Review the story, "Tales About Tails."

b. While Beaver and Muskrat bragged about their tails, Otter caught ten fish. Find page 219 in the *Student Activity Book* and cut out the fish for **2b**. Ask your student to copy these number words on the fish, and put them in order: one two three four five six seven eight nine ten.

c. Remind your student that a compound word is two words joined together to make a new word. Find page 219 in the *Student Activity Book*. Cut out the word cards for **2c**. Read the words with your student. Ask him to make four new words and read them to you. **everywhere, nowhere, somewhere, anywhere**

d. Read the passage with your student.

> *"I can cut a stick in two with my tail," said Muskrat. "Can you?"*
> *"Of course I can," said Beaver. "And I can cut a tree down with my tail,"* Beaver said. *"Can you?"*
> *Otter came along the shore. He carried his fishing pole on his shoulder.*

Remind your student that **ou** can say **/ow/** as in *out*. Tell him that **ou** can also say **/ō/** as in *your*. Look at the second line of the passage with your student. Ask him to find the word in which **ou** says **/ō/** as in *court*. **course** If he can not, then just tell him. Ask him to the find the word in the last sentence in which **ou** says **/ō/** as in *your*. **shoulder**

Read these words with your student: *four pour court source*.

Ask him to make up a sentence with each word orally.

e. How Do You Spell That Word?

Give your student a piece of paper and a pencil. Dictate the spelling words to your student, guiding him through the process and helping him learn spelling rules. Review the following as needed.
1) *knot - Sometimes the /n/ sound at the beginning of a word is spelled* **kn**.
2) *know - Same as 1. Sometimes the /o/ sound is spelled* **ow** *at the end of a word.*
3) *knit* - Same as 1.
4) *knife* - Same as 1.

Day 3

a. Review the story, "Tales About Tails."

b. Remind your student that the words *two*, *too*, and *to* are homonyms, words that often sound the same, have a different meaning, and usually a different spelling. Tell your student that our story contains a homonym in the title, "Tales About Tails." Look at the title of the story with your student. Ask him to tell you the meanings of both words. Ask him to point to the word which means a story, and spell it for you. **tales** Ask him to point to the word which means the body part of an animal, and spell it for you. **tails**

c. Ask your student to write the correct words to complete the sentences.

1) I have **two** dimes in my pocket.
2) I woke up **too** late.
3) Please come **to** my house.
4) The pig has a curly **tail**.
5) Dad will tell us a funny **tale**.

d. Context Word: once

I rode the bike *once* around the block.

e. Syllable Sense: Ask your student to divide these words using the rules learned. Ask him to read the words aloud. Your student can clap as he says the words to help him hear the syllables. **be/gan a/long be/hind o/ver**.

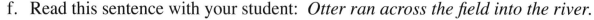

f. Read this sentence with your student: *Otter ran across the field into the river.*

Look at the word *field* with your student. Say the word and ask him to repeat it. Ask him what sound **ie** makes in the word. **/ē/ sound** Tell your student that **ie** usually says /ē/ as in *field*.

Read these words with your student: *piece thief believe chief cookie carried.*

Use these words from the Phonics Word Box to fill in the following sentences:

1) The word **thief** rhymes with **chief**.
2) We baked a big **cookie** today.
3) I would like a **piece** of pie.
4) Do you **believe** that story?

g. Ask your student to complete the Spelling Words Puzzle.
  1) **knife** 2) **knot** 3) **knit** 4) **know**

h. Find page 217 in the *Student Activity Book* and ask your student to trace the sentence on the top.

Day 4

a. Review the Word List below for "Tales About Tails."

| course | shoulder | carried | caught | once |
| climbed | began | behind | over | along |

b. Read these sentences with your student.

  Beaver caught some fish. He taught Otter how to cook it. Beaver cooked it in sauce.

Point to the word *sauce* in the last sentence. Say the word aloud and ask your student to repeat it. Tell him that **au** says /**aw**/ as in *sauce*.

c. Read these words with your student: *cause pause fault sauce haul maul.* Ask him to fill in the blank with the correct word.

1) We need to **haul** that wood to the pile.
2) I'm sorry. This was my **fault**.
3) Mom makes the best cheese **sauce**.
4) A sharp pin may **cause** pain.

d. Now, point to the word *caught* in the first sentence. Ask your student to circle it. Say the word aloud and ask your student to repeat it. Tell him that in this word, **au** says /aw/ and the **gh** is silent. Show him the word *taught* in the second sentence and repeat the process.

e. Read the words in the Phonics Word Box with your student: *naughty   taught   caught   daughter*.

   Ask him to fill in the blanks with the correct word.

   1) I **caught** the ball.
   2) My teacher **taught** me how to read.
   3) Mary is her **daughter**.

f. Help your student number a piece of paper 1 - 4. Dictate the spelling words to your student. If he has any difficulty at all, use the same process used in **2e**.

g. Find page 217 in the *Student Activity Book* and ask your student to copy the sentence on the bottom line and color the page. He may take two days to complete this assignment.

Day 5

a. Ask your student to read "Tales About Tails" aloud.

b. Read these sentences with your student.

   Muskrat has a long, thin tail. Beaver has a short, flat tail.

   Ask your student what kind of tail Muskrat has. Underline these describing words. **long, thin tail** Ask him what kind of tail Beaver has. Underline these words. **short, flat tail**

   Sometimes a naming word or noun has more than one word describing it. When two or more describing words come before the noun, use commas to separate those describing words. Ask your student to circle the commas in the sentences above. **long, thin tail   short, flat tail**

   Ask your student to add commas to the following sentences:

   1) Beaver chewed on the big , thick branch.
   2) Muskrat lay on the old , rotten log.
   3) Otter swam in the clean , cool water.

c. Read this sentence to your student: *See Muskrat climb out of the water.*

Ask your student to look at the word *climb* and circle it. Say the word and ask your student to tell you the silent letter. **the letter b** Ask him to cross it out.

Tell your student that several words end with **m** and a silent **b**. Read the words in the Phonics Word Box with your student: *climbed lamb comb tomb limb bomb dumb*. Tell your student that when **-ed** or **-ing** is added to the end of a word like *climb*, the **b** remains silent.

Ask him to choose the correct word to fill in the blanks.

1) I have to **comb** my hair.
2) Don **climbed** the trees.
3) He has a swing on the **limb** of the tree.
4) The **lamb** has white fur.

d. Optional: Spelling test

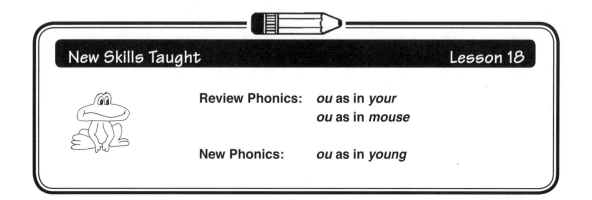

Day 1

a. Find the story, "Five Times Ten," in the reader, *In, Out, and About Catfish Pond*. Read it to or with your student.

b. Talk to your student about the story. You may use these questions to help you in your discussion.

1) *Duck has done something very unkind to Turtle What did she do, and why was it wrong?* **Duck told Turtle's secret. Turtle trusted Duck not to tell anyone, and Duck betrayed her confidence.**

2) *Not only did Duck break her promise to Turtle, but every time she told someone else, she asked him not to tell Turtle about her mistake. That put Turtle's friends in an uncomfortable position.*

3) *How did Turtle know that Duck had told her secret?* **Muskrat gave her a fish cake with five times ten candles. Beaver and Otter gave her ten times five lilies.**

4) *How did Turtle feel when she saw her friends?* **She felt embarrassed and was upset at Duck.**

5) *Has someone ever shared a secret you asked him not to tell? How did you feel?*

6) *There are some things we like to keep secret, like what we got someone for a birthday present, or when a surprise party is planned. There are other things that we should not keep a secret, like when something wrong has been done, or if someone has said or done something bad to you. Talk with your student about secrets that are all right, and secrets that are not. Ask him to think of a example of each kind of secret to make sure he understands.*

Materials needed:
In, Out, and About Catfish Pond

Little Island by Golden MacDonald

c. Read the passage with your student.

> *"Today is Turtle's birthday," Duck said.*

Show your student the apostrophe **s** (**'s**) in the word *Turtle's*. Ask him when he has used an apostrophe before. **possessive nouns and contractions** Apostrophe and **s** are used to show ownership or possession. The *birthday* in the sentence belongs to Turtle; it is Turtle's birthday.

A house which belongs to Muskrat would be called *Muskrat's house*. Ask your student to write the possessive form using an apostrophe and **s**. Ex: the house belonging to Muskrat - Muskrat's house

1) the rock belonging to Turtle **Turtle's rock**
2) the secret belonging to Duck **Duck's secret**
3) the hat belonging to Beaver **Beaver's hat**

d. Review with your student that **ou** can say /ō/ as in *court*. Ask your student to read the words in the Phonics Word Box: *pour   court   four   shoulder*.

Ask your student to complete the following sentences with one of the words.
1) Two plus two is **four**.
2) Mom will **pour** the milk.
3) The judge is in **court**.
4) Grandma put a blanket on her **shoulder**.

e. Ask your student to copy the spelling words for this week. Read them to or with your student: *four   pour   piece   sauce*.

f. Ask your student to look at the picture of Turtle's birthday cake. Draw five rows, with ten candles in each row. How old is Turtle on her birthday? **50** Ask your student to write the number of candles in the blank.

Day 2

a. Review the story, "Five Times Ten."

b. Find page 229 in the *Student Activity Book*. Ask your student to cut out the pictures for **2b**, put them in the correct order, and glue them on blank paper. He may write or dictate sentences for each picture.

c. Ask your student to make compound words using the Word List.
   birthday, afternoon, catfish

d. Tell your student that **ou** usually says /**ow**/ as in *out*, but it can also say /**ŭ**/ as in *young*. Read the words in the Phonics Word Box with your student: *house young country touch double trouble sound cloud mouse.*

   Ask your student to fill in the blanks with the best word.

   1) There was a loud **sound** just now.
   2) My aunt has a farm in the **country**.
   3) The sky has a big fluffy **cloud** in it today.
   4) Do not **touch** the stove. It is hot.
   5) There is a cute little **mouse** in our **house**.
   6) The kittens are still too **young** to leave their mother.

e. How Do You Spell That Word?

   Give your student a piece of paper and a pencil. Dictate the spelling words to your student, guiding him through the process.
   1) *four - The /ō/ sound in the middle of a word may be spelled **ou**.*
   2) *pour - Same as 1.*
   3) *sauce - The /aw/ sound may be spelled **au** in the middle of a word.*
   4) *piece - The /e/ sound may be spelled **ie**.*

Day 3

a. Review the story, "Five Times Ten."

b. Read these sentences with your student. Ask him to tell you the doing word in each sentence and circle it. Then ask him to act it out.

   1) Turtle **stretched** in the sun.
   2) Duck **shook** her wings.
   3) Muskrat **swam** in the pond.

c. Context Word: gone.
   I went outside to find my cat, but he was *gone*.

d. Syllable Sense: Ask your student to divide these words and read them aloud.
   se/cret in/deed fig/ure nev/er

e. Ask your student to complete the Spelling Words Puzzle.

CODE									
a	c	e	f	i	o	p	r	s	u
1	2	3	4	5	6	7	8	9	10

"You may **p o u r** a drink and get a **p i e c e** of pizza, Jack," said Mom.
      7 6 10 8   7 5 3 2 3

"Mom, this pizza **s a u c e** is great. I could eat **f o u r** pieces," said Jack.
              9 1 10 2 3   4 6 10 8

f. Find page 228 in the *Student Activity Book* and ask your student to trace the sentence on the top.

Day 4

a. Review the Word List below for "Five Times Ten."

young	*gone*	*secret*	*indeed*
figure	*never*	*myself*	*afternoon*

b. Review with your student that a sentence has two parts:

1) The subject tells who or what the sentence is about.
2) The predicate tells something about the subject.

Using the three sentences from **3b**, ask your student to underline the subject, or who or what the sentence is about. Then double underline the part that tells something about the subject.
1) <u>Turtle</u> <u>stretched in the sun.</u>
2) <u>Duck</u> <u>shook her wings.</u>
3) <u>Muskrat</u> <u>swam in the pond.</u>

c. Read the book, *Little Island*, by Golden MacDonald to your student, or he may read it to you.

d. Talk to your student about the story. You may use these questions to help you in your discussion.

1) *The Island in our story is little, but important. Why do you think the Island is important.* **Island provided life for creatures and plants.**
2) *Can you remember what animals visited the Island?* Tell me. **Birds, fish, spiders, lobsters, seals, kingfishers, gulls, herring, mackerel, crow, bat, owl, kitten**

3) *Look at the pictures and tell me about your favorite picture. What do you like about it?*

e. Help your student number a piece of paper 1 - 4. Dictate the spelling words to your student. If he has any difficulty at all, use the same process used in **2e**.

f. Find page 228 in the *Student Activity Book* and ask your student to copy the sentence on the bottom line and color the page. He may take two days to complete this assignment.

Day 5

a. Ask your student to read "Five Times Ten" aloud. Celebrate his success and add to his Reading Chart.

b. Read this sentence with your student.

One day, Muskrat was fixing the door on his house.

Remind your student that a noun names a person, place, or thing. Ask your student to circle all the nouns in the sentence. **day, Muskrat, door, house**

Ask him to tell you why Muskrat begins with a capital letter. Proper nouns begin with a capital letter. The name of a particular person, place, or thing begins with a capital letter. These words are called proper nouns. Ask your student to write down all the proper nouns found in the story. **Muskrat, Turtle, Duck, Beaver, Otter**

c. Research an island. Choose one of these or another island you find on a map.

Australia	New Zealand	Cayman
Greenland	Borneo	Cuba

Use an encyclopedia or atlas to learn about the island. You may use the following questions to help you.
1) What type of weather is on this island?
2) What type of animals live on this island?
3) What do the people do on this island?
4) What sounds interesting to you about this island?
5) Would you like to go to this island? Why or why not?

Ask your student to draw a picture on page 229 of the *Student Activity Book* of the island he researched. Include anything of interest in his picture.

d. Optional: Spelling test

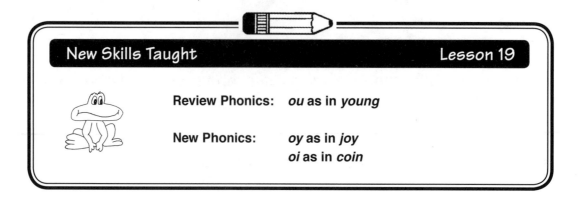

Review Phonics: *ou* as in *young*

New Phonics: *oy* as in *joy*
                  oi as in *coin*

Materials needed:
In, Out, and About Catfish Pond

Billy and Blaze by C.W. Anderson

Day 1

a. Find the story, "Muskrat's Fishing Hat." Read it to or with your student.

b. Talk to your student about the story. You may use these questions to help you in your discussion.

　1) *Tell me the story using your own words. You may use the pictures to help you.*
　2) *What do you think Muskrat has done that is wrong?* **He jumped to a conclusion accusing Beaver of taking his hat**.
　3) *What did Otter and Duck do that was wrong?* **They mistrusted Beaver just because of Muskrat's accusation**.
　4) *What did Beaver say when Otter and Duck talked to him?* **Beaver said he did not take Muskrat's hat.**
　5) *Have you ever been falsely accused of doing something? How did it make you feel? Tell me about it.*
　6) *Beaver did not seem to be angry with Muskrat. What kind of an attitude did Beaver have?* **Beaver was wise, understanding, and patient.**
　7) *Why is it hurtful to tell something that isn't true about someone? What can some of the consequences be?*
　8) *What do you think it means to forgive someone?* **It means to no longer hold them accountable for a wrong action.**

c. Read the passage with your student.

　　"What a day for fishing!" Muskrat said. He put on his fishing pants. He picked up his fishing box. He reached in the closet for his green fishing hat. But the hat was not there.

Show your student that the actual words spoken by Muskrat are enclosed by quotation marks. Read it to or with your student. *What a day for fishing!*

Tell him that the quotation marks tell us the actual words spoken. Ask him to circle the quotation marks. Ask him to act out the passage, using some props and saying his line, "What a day for fishing!"

d. Read this passage with your student.

> *"I cannot go fishing without my hat," Muskrat said. He looked under the bed. He looked behind the door. But the hat was not there.*

Do the same as in **1c** above.

e. Review with your student that **ou** can say /ŭ/ as in *young*. Read the words in the Phonics Word Box with your student: *country touch young trouble.*

Ask your student to look at the picture, read each sentence, and put an X next to the sentence that best describes the picture.

___1) The young lady sat down.
___2) May I touch the bushes in your yard?
 X 3) My grandma lives in the country.
___4) He caused her some trouble.

f. Ask your student to copy the spelling words for this week. Read them to or with your student: *shout touch come could.*

Day 2

a. Review the story, "Muskrat's Fishing Hat."

b. Under the picture of each character ask your student to list words that describe him in this story. He may use the reader and copy the words.
Muskrat - small head, narrow head, sorry   Beaver - honest, large head, fat head

c. Remind your student that the words enclosed in quotation marks (" ") are the words actually spoken by someone. Read these sentences with your student. Ask him to underline the actual words spoken.
1) **"<u>Someone has taken my fishing hat!</u>"** Muskrat shouted.
2) **"<u>Who would take your fishing hat?</u>"** Otter asked.
3) Muskrat patted his head with his paw. **"<u>It must be Beaver,</u>"** Muskrat said.

d. How Do You Spell That Word?

Give your student a piece of paper and a pencil. Dictate the spelling words to your student, guiding him through the process. Review the following as needed.

1) *shout - The /ow/ sound in the middle of a word can be spelled* **ou**.
2) *come - This is a common word.* Spell it for him if needed.
3) *could -* Same as 2.
4) *touch - The /ŭ/ sound in the middle of a word may be spelled* **ou**.

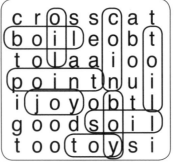

e. Read these sentences with your student.

> *Muskrat had no joy because he could not find his fishing hat.*
> *Duck pointed a wing at Beaver. She said "You have taken Muskrat's fishing hat."*

Show your student the word *joy.* Ask him to circle it. Tell him that **oy** says **/oi/** as in *joy*. Read the words in the Phonics Word Box with your student. Ask him to copy the words, saying the words aloud as he writes them: *joy toy boy Roy Troy.*

Ask your student to look at the word *pointed*. Ask him to circle it. Say the word aloud and ask your student to repeat it. Ask him if he can tell you the two letters which make up the **/oi/** sound. **oi** Ask him to turn to page 234 in his *Student Activity Book.* Read the words in the Phonics Word Box with your student. Ask him to copy the words, saying the words aloud as he writes them: *point boil oil coin soil.*

f. Ask your student to complete the Word Search Puzzle with some of the words above. Ask him to read the words he circled. If he has trouble finding the **oi** and **oy** words, show him the words.

g. Ask your student to tell you what *doubt* means. Use a dictionary if needed. Discuss how Muskrat's accusations about Beaver caused doubt for Duck and Otter about Beaver's character. Ask your student to write or dictate a letter to Muskrat telling him how damaging it is to accuse someone without proof of wrong-doing.

Day 3

a. Review the story, "Muskrat's Fishing Hat."

b. Read the passage with your student.

> *"Beaver seems like an honest fellow. I let him take care of my house when I was away last fall," Otter said. "I always trusted Beaver. But maybe I was wrong."*

Review with your student that a noun is a word which names a person, place, or thing. It is often awkward to name the same noun over and over again, so we use pronouns. Ask your student to listen to the same passage using nouns instead of pronouns.

> *"Beaver seems like an honest fellow. Otter let Beaver take care of Otter's house when Otter was away last fall," Otter said. "Otter always trusted Beaver. But maybe Otter was wrong."*

Ask your student which way sounds better. Tell him he uses pronouns everyday when he talks, but he may not have noticed it.

c. Read the passage and ask your student to circle the pronouns.

> *Muskrat shook (his) fur. "(I) know Beaver has (my) hat," (he) said.*

d. Context Words: *honest   closet   guess*

1) Mary tells the truth. She is an *honest* person.
2) I keep my coat in the *closet*.
3) I don't know the answer, but I will *guess* it.

e. Syllable Sense: Ask your student to divide these words and read them aloud.
un/der   af/ter   o/pened   ta/ken   go/ing   duck/lings

f. Ask your student to complete the Spelling Words Puzzle.
1) **could**   2) **shout**   3) **touch**   4) **come**

g. Find page 238 in the *Student Activity Book* and ask your student to trace the sentence on the top.

Day 4

a. Review the Word List below for "Muskrat's Fishing Hat."

pointed   *honest*   *closet*   *guess*   *ducklings*   *going*   *yourself*

b. Read the book, *Billy and Blaze*, by C.W. Anderson. Talk to your student about the story. You may use the following questions to help you in your discussion.

1) *Do you like the name Billy gave his pony? What would you have named him?*
2) *Do you think Billy loved Blaze? How did Billy show his love?* **He took good care of him.**
3) *What responsibilities did Billy have in taking care of Blaze and Rex?* **playing with them, cleaning them, feeding them, etc.**

c. Review with your student that when two words are joined together to make a contraction, an apostrophe is used to show where the letter (s) have been left out. Review the following contractions with your student by reading the contraction and the two words which make up the contraction. Tell him the missing letters. Ask him to cross out the missing letters.

1) didn't - **did not**   3) he's - **he is** *or* **he has**
2) haven't - **have not**   4) she'll - **she will**

Ask your student to tell you or write the words for which each contraction stands.

5) doesn't - **does not**   7) you're - **you are**
6) isn't - **is not**   8) it's - **it is** *or* **it has**

d. Help your student number a piece of paper 1 - 4. Dictate the spelling words to your student. If he has any difficulty at all, use the same process used in **2d**.

e. Find page 238 in the *Student Activity Book* and ask your student to copy the sentence on the bottom line and color the page. He may take two days to complete this assignment.

f. Ask your student to fold a piece of paper in half and make two columns, one marked *Blaze* and one marked *Rex*. Ask your student to think of things Billy would do for each animal and write them in the correct column. Your student may think of other ways to care for them, and add them to the list.

Day 5

a. Ask your student to read "Muskrat's Fishing Hat" aloud. Celebrate his success and add to his Reading Chart.

b. Ask your student to look at the title of our story: "Muskrat's Fishing Hat." Ask him to circle the apostrophe **s**. Ask him why he thinks an apostrophe **s** ('**s**) is placed after *Muskrat*. **to show possession or ownership   The fishing hat belongs to Muskrat.**

Ask your student to write the possessive form for the following.
Ex: the tail belonging to Beaver -- Beaver's tail

1) the fishing pants belonging to Muskrat **Muskrat's fishing pants**
2) the face belonging to Beaver **Beaver's face**
3) the wings belonging to Duck **Duck's wings**

c. On page 46 of the reader, Beaver describes his head. What describing words does he use? **large and fat** Beaver then describes Muskrat's head. What describing words does he use?   **small and narrow**

d. Find page 239 in the *Student Activity Book*. Find the hats that belong to Beaver, Duck, Muskrat, and Otter. Decorate and color these hats to match their personalities. There is no right or wrong way to do this. Allow your student to interpret his feelings about each character.

e. Optional: Spelling test

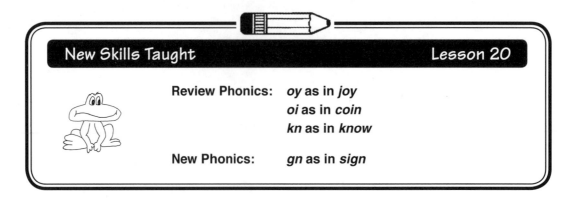

New Skills Taught   **Lesson 20**

Review Phonics: *oy* as in *joy*
                        oi as in *coin*
                        kn as in *know*

New Phonics: *gn* as in *sign*

Materials needed:
   In, Out, and About
   Catfish Pond

   craft materials

Day 1

a. Find the story, "The Pond Monster," in the reader, *In, Out, and About Catfish Pond.* Read it to or with your student.

b. Talk to your student about the story. You may use the following questions to help you in your discussion.

   1) *Sometimes people get upset with the things we do. Some things may upset friends or people in your family. How can you be thoughtful and helpful towards your friends and family?*

   2) *Who was upset in our story?* **Turtle** *How did Turtle feel and what did she do?* **She thought people were intentionally disturbing her, and she did something to try to make them go away.**

   3) *What finally helped the Pond animals understand what Turtle wanted?* **She made a loud noise, and she explained her frustrations to them.**

   4) *What mistake did Turtle make in the way she let her feelings be known?* **She wasn't honest with them.** *What would have been a better way for Turtle to share her feelings?* **Turtle could have told the truth.**

   5) *Have you ever let your feelings be known in a wrong way? How did you express your anger? Do you think people are always trying to anger us like we might imagine?*

   6) *How can you respond to someone who has shared something that bothers him?* **Read Matthew 7:12 to your student.**

c. Ask your student to tell you a word which means the opposite of *hot*. **cold** Words of opposite meanings are called antonyms. Here are some words from our story. Read the word aloud to your student, and ask him to tell you an antonym, or a word of opposite meaning.

1) *closed* - **opened**   4) *over* - **under**
2) *out* - **in**   5) *loud* - **quiet**
3) *near* - **far**

d. Read the words in the Phonics Word Box with your student: *boil coin boy toy*.

Ask your student to complete the following sentences using these words.

1) Mother will **boil** the water.   2) I broke my **toy**.
3) I put a **coin** in my piggy bank.   4) The little **boy** played.

e. Ask your student to copy the spelling words for this week. Read them to or with your student: *boy toy soil coin*.

f. Find page 243 in the *Student Activity Book*. Ask your student to cut out the word cards. Read the words with him. Ask him to match the words with opposite meanings, glue them on blank paper, and illustrate three of them. **open-close, good-bad, fast-slow, short-tall, night-day, old-young, black-white, up-down, heavy-light**

Day 2

a. Review the story, "The Pond Monster," with your student.

b. Look through the story with your student for *sound words*, such as *splash*, *clop-clop*, and *rrrrrraaaaaaa*. Notice how they look compared to the other words. Ask him why he thinks they are typed differently and what each one means.

c. Review with your student that a sentence has two parts:
   1) the subject, or who or what the sentence is about
   2) the predicate, the part that tells something about the subject

Read these sentences with your student. Ask him to underline the subject once, and double underline the predicate, the part that tells something about the subject.

1) **The sun was halfway behind the willow trees.**
2) **The noise came from Turtle's shell.**
3) **Otter stopped hitting the water with his tail.**

Teacher's Note: The word *half way* **may be spelled** *half way* **or** *halfway.*

d. How Do You Spell That Word?

Give your student a piece of paper and a pencil. Dictate the spelling words to your student, helping him learn spelling rules. Review the following as needed.

1) *coin - The /oy/ sound is often spelled* **oi** *in the middle of a word.*
2) *boy - The /oy/ sound is often spelled* **oy** *at the end of a word; never* **oi.**
3) *soil - Same as 1.*
4) *toy - Same as 2.*

e. Read the passage with your student.

> *"I'm sorry," said Turtle. The next day she put a sign on her rock.*

Your student has learned that **kn** says **/n/** as in *knee*. Ask him to tell you the silent letter. **k**

Tell your student that **gn** can also say **/n/**. Ask him to tell you the silent letter. **g** Ask your student to find the **gn** word in the passage and circle it. **sign**

Read the words in the Phonics Word Box with your student: *sign gnaw gnat design.*

Ask your student to fill in the blanks with the correct word.

1) Her dress has a pretty **design** on it.
2) We will meet you at the stop **sign**.
3) There is a little **gnat** flying near me.
4) The king will **gnaw** on the turkey leg.

Day 3

a. Review the story, "The Pond Monster," with your student.

b. Read these sentences with your student.

> *Turtle put a bag over her head. Turtle made an awful noise. The noise was very loud.*

Review with your student that the little words *a*, *an*, and *the* tell us that a naming word is coming. The first sentence tells us that Turtle put *a* bag over her head. This means she put **any** bag over her head, not a *particular* bag. The second sentence tells us that Turtle made an awful noise. This means she made *any* awful noise.

Tell your student to use the words *a* and *an* when referring to any one of many things. Use *a* with a word beginning with a consonant sound; use *an* with a word beginning with a vowel sound.

Ask your student to write *a* or *an* in each blank.

1) **an** apple
2) **a** bag
3) **an** ear
4) **a** rock

The third sentence tells us that *the* noise was very loud. This refers to the particular noise that Turtle made.

c. Context Words: *half thought*.

   1) I can't eat a whole pizza, but I can eat *half*.
   2) I was unhappy about the game. I *thought* it was going to be better.

d. Syllable Sense: **a/fraid a/gain dis/turb**

e. Ask your student to complete the Spelling Words Puzzle.
   1) We plant seeds in the **soil**.   3) A dime is a **coin**.
   2) Jack is a **boy** in my class.   4) He got a **toy** truck for his birthday.

f. Find page 247 in the *Student Activity Book* and ask your student to trace the sentence on the top.

Day 4

a. Review the Word List below for "The Pond Monster."

sign   half   thought   afraid   disturb   again   hardly

b. Look through the reader, *In, Out, and About Catfish Pond.* Talk to your student about the characters, stories, and setting. You may use these questions to help you in your discussion.

1) *Choose a character from the reader. Find parts of the reader that show what type of personality he/she has in the reader. Ex: Otter is a caring friend. See page 8.*
2) *Which characters and stories did you like? Why?*
3) *What do you like about the pictures?*
4) *Can you find the page that tells us the page number on which each story begins?*
5) *Can you find the page that tells us who wrote these stories and who illustrated them?*

c. Read this passage with your student.

   "There's a monster over there!"

Review with your student that a contraction is two words joined together with an apostrophe. Ask your student to find the contraction in this passage. Ask your student to copy it. **there's** Now, write the words the contraction stands for: **there is**. Ask him to cross out the letter(s) which the apostrophe replaces. **letter i** Continue the same process with these contractions.

1) what's - **what is OR what has**
2) here's - **here is**
3) where's - **where is OR where has**

d. Find pages 249 in the *Student Activity Book.* There are several pictures of characters from *In, Out, and About Catfish Pond.* Discuss these Catfish Pond projects with your student and ask him to choose one to work on today and tomorrow.

1) Color and cut out the pictures. Use a box to create a 3-D scene, or diorama, of the Catfish Pond. Your student can write or dictate a summary of a few stories or make up his own.

2) Color and cut out the pictures, glue each picture on a piece of blank paper and ask your student to write or dictate a sentence for each one.

    3) Create a new story about the characters. Staple several pages together. Write the story in the book and glue the pictures as desired. Color the pictures. Title your story.

  e. Help your student number a piece of paper 1 - 4. Dictate the spelling words to your student. If he has any difficulty at all, use the same process used in **2d**.

  f. Find page 247 in the *Student Activity Book* and ask your student to copy the sentence on the bottom line and color the page. He may take two days to complete this assignment.

Day 5

  a. Ask your student to read "The Pond Monster" aloud. Celebrate his success and add to his Reading Chart. Your student has now completed *In, Out, and About Catfish Pond*. Add this book cover to his Reading Chart.

  b. Continue to work on the Catfish Pond project.

  c. Prepare to present it to a group.

  d. Optional: Spelling test

  e. Today, complete *Assessment 4* with your student.

Assessment 4
(Lessons 16 - 20)

This is the oral part of Assessment 4.

1. *Antonyms are words of opposite meaning. Tell me an antonym for these words.*

   a. *big* - **Possible answers: little, small**
   b. *pretty* - **Possible answers: ugly, messy**
   c. *happy* - **Possible answers: sad, unhappy**
   d. *tall* - **Possible answer: short**

2. *A common noun is a word that names any person, place, or thing. A proper noun is a word that names a particular person, place, or thing. Tell me if these words are common nouns or proper nouns.*

   a. *dog* **common**
   b. *William* **proper**
   c. *city* **common**
   d. *country* **common**
   e. *New York* **proper**

3. *A pronoun is a word that takes place of a noun. Tell me a pronoun to replace the noun in these sentences.*

   a. *My parents are not home. <u>My parents</u> are on vacation. What pronoun can replace* My parents? **They**
   b. *Marcy forgot <u>Marcy's</u> coat. What pronoun can replace* Marcy's? **her**
   c. *Todd and Will are brothers. <u>Todd and Will</u> are my cousins. What pronoun can replace* Todd and Will? **They**

The following is the written part of Assessment 4. Find page 251 in his *Student Activity Book*, and ask him to complete it as you instruct him.

1. *Add **-ly** to these words.*

   a. slow - **slowly**
   b. glad - **gladly**
   c. sad - **sadly**

2. *The words* too, to, *and* two *are homonyms. Write the correct word for each sentence.*

   a. I have **two** cookies.
   b. I will give one cookie **to** my friend.
   c. I ate **too** many cookies.

3. *The words* a *and* an *are words that tell us a naming word, or noun, is coming. Write* a *or* an *in the blanks.*

   a. **a** butterfly
   b. **a** horse
   c. **an** octopus
   d. **an** eel

4. *A sentence has two parts: the subject, or who or what the sentence is about; and the predicate, the part that tells something about the subject. Underline who or what the sentence is about. Double underline the part that tells something about the subject.*

   a. **Stacy and Kelly laughed.**
   b. **Stacy rolled on the grass**.
   c. **Kelly jumped over the fence**.

5. *Add* **-ed** *to these words.*

   a. hope   **hoped**
   b. like   **liked**
   c. save   **saved**

6. *Add* **-ing** *to these words.*

   a. skip   **skipping**
   b. sit   **sitting**
   c. put   **putting**
   d. eat   **eating**
   e. sing   **singing**

7. *Quotation marks tell us that someone is speaking. Underline the words that are spoken.*

   Jamie said, "I will come today."

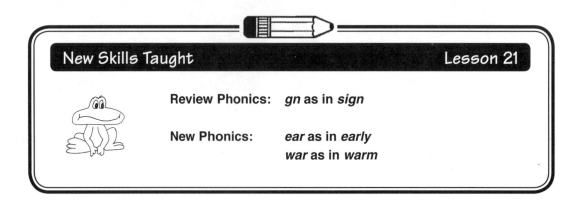

Materials needed:
Up, Down, and Around the Rain Tree

Day 1

a. Find the story, "Parrot's Many Troubles" in the reader *Up, Down, and Around the Rain Tree*. Read it to or with your student.

b. Talk to your student about the story. You may use these questions to help you in your discussion.

1) *What did Parrot do when everyone was asleep?* **He picked nuts.**
2) *Do you think Parrot picked just enough nuts for himself or do you think he picked too many? Why or why not?* **Allow for discussion.**
3) *What were Parrot's many troubles?* **He could not sleep because he had nuts everywhere; he also ate too many nuts.**
4) *What did Monkey do for Parrot?* **He fixed warm milk.**
5) *Do you think Parrot learned anything from his "many troubles"?* **Allow for discussion.**

c. A word that could be used to describe Parrot's behavior is *greedy*. Look up this word in a dictionary and read the definition to your student. Talk with him about whether he thinks this word applies to Parrot.

d. Talk to your student about attitudes about sharing. Should we let others go first, or let them take the best of something? It may not be easy to let others go ahead of you. Ask your student to think of a situation when he let someone else go first or take the best of something. How did he feel afterward?

e. Read the words in the Phonics Word Box with your student: *sign gnaw design reign*

Ask him to complete these sentences.

1) Dad will **sign** his name.
2) The beaver will **gnaw** on the tree.
3) The paper has a pretty **design**.
4) The king will **reign** over the country.

f. Ask your student to copy the spelling words for this week. Read them to or with your student: *sign gnat some said*.

Day 2

a. Review the story, "Parrot's Many Troubles," with your student.

b. Talk to your student about Parrot.

1) *How did he act at the beginning of the story?*
2) *How did he act at the end of the story?*
3) *Why do you think he changed during the story?*

Ask your student to look at the pictures and write or dictate phrases that describe Parrot during these parts of the story.

c. Read the passage with your student.

> *Picking nuts made him sleepy. But Parrot could not sleep. The nuts under his pillow were hard. They felt bumpy. Parrot got up. The nuts under the rug were hard. They felt lumpy.*

Ask your student to underline the word *sleepy*. Circle the letter **y** at the end of the word.

The word *sleepy* is made from the base word *sleep* with the suffix **y** added to it.

Ask your student for the base word of *bumpy* and *lumpy*. **bump, lump** Adding the suffix **y** to these kinds of words are easy. Ask your student to add **y** to these words and say the base word and the new word aloud.

1) dirt - **dirty** 2) chunk - **chunky** 3) dust - **dusty** 4) rain - **rainy**

d. Read the passage with your student.

> *He pulled a nut off the branch. He broke it open with his beak. "Ummm, very tasty."*

Ask your student to underline the word *tasty*. Circle the letter **y**. Show your student the base word of *tasty*: taste. Tell him that if a word ends with a silent **e**, you must drop the **e** before adding the **y**. Ask your student to add **y** to these words by dropping the silent **e**. Say the base word and the new word aloud.
1) shine - **shiny** 2) bone - **bony** 3) slime - **slimy** 4) grease - **greasy**

e. Read this passage with your student.

> *"You are too late," Parrot said.*
> *"You got here too early," Monkey said.*

Your student has learned the three most common ways of spelling the **/er/** sound: **er, ir**, and **ur**. Ask your student to read the second sentence in the passage, and ask him to circle the word that makes an **/er/** sound. Show him that *early* is spelled **e-a-r-l-y**. The letters **ear** also makes an **/er/** sound.

Read this passage with your student.

> *Outside Monkey heard Parrot's cries.*

Again, ask your student what word in the passage makes an **/er/** sound. Circle the word. **heard**

Read the words in the Phonics Word Box with your student:
early earth earn heard learn pearl search.

Ask him to fill in the blanks with the correct word from the Phonics Word Box.

1) I lost my book. I have to **search** for it.
2) I do not know how to knit. I want to **learn**.
3) I can not be late. I have to wake up early.
4) My mom has a **pearl** necklace.

f. How Do You Spell That Word?

Give your student a piece of paper and a pencil. Dictate the spelling words to your student, guiding him through the process.

1) *some* - This is a common word; help your student as needed.
2) *sign* - *The /n/ sound may be spelled* **gn** *at the end of a word.*
3) *said* - Same as 1.
4) *gnat* - Same as 2.

Day 3

a. Review the story for this week.

b. Read the passage with your student.

> *Parrot emptied his sack. He hid some nuts under his pillow. He hid some nuts under the rug.*

Show your student the base word of *emptied*: empty. Tell your student that Parrot will empty his sack today, and he emptied it yesterday. When something has already been done, we say it is in the past tense.

Words like *empty* which end with a consonant and **y**, must change the **y** to **i** before adding **-ed**. Ask your student to add **-ed** to these words by changing the **y** to **i**.

Teacher's Note: This rule is true for words with both the /ē/ sound and /ī/ sound of y.

1) hurry - **hurried**   2) carry - **carried**   3) fry - **fried**   4) try - **tried**   5) cry - **cried**

c. You have learned in **3b** that words ending with a consonant and **y** must change the **y** to **i** before adding **-ed**. Look at the word *empty* and *empties*. Ask him if he can tell you the rule for adding **s** to words ending with a consonant and **y**. If he doesn't know, tell him that words that end with a consonant **y**, must change the **y** to **i** and then add **es**. Ask your student to add **s** to these words by changing the **y** to **i,** and adding **-es**.
1) hurry - **hurries**   2) carry - **carries**   3) fry - **fries**   4) try - **tries**   5) cry - **cries**

d. Read the passage with your student.

> *"Thank you, Monkey," Parrot replied. "You are kind."*

Show your student the word *replied*, and ask him to underline it. The letters **ie** can say /ĭ/ as in *replied*.

Ask your student to read the words in the Phonics Word Box: *tried fried cried*.

e. Read the passage with your student.

> *Parrot looked around. Everyone was asleep.*

Ask your student to look at the word *everyone*. Two words joined together to make a new word is called a compound word. Ask your student to tell you the two words which make up the compound word. Draw a line between the two words.
every / one

f. Find page 243 in the *Student Activity Book*. Cut out all the word cards for **3f**. Ask your student to make as many compound words as he can using the word *every*.
everyone, everywhere, everyday, everything

g. Context Words: *stomach through full pulled*.

   1) I ate too much. My *stomach* is *full*.
   2) We played tug of war. I *pulled* as hard as I could pull.
   3) We drove *through* the tunnel.

h. Ask your student to complete the Spelling Words Puzzle.
1) some 2) gnat 3) said 4) sign

i. Find page 261 in the *Student Activity Book* and ask your student to trace the sentence on the top of the page.

Day 4

a. Review the Word List below for "Parrot's Many Troubles."

early	*heard*	*replied*	*cries*	*cried*	*warm*
stomach	*through*	*full*	*pulled*	*tasty*	

b. Read the passage with your student.

He began to pick the nuts. He picked the biggest nuts first.

Ask your student to circle the word *biggest*. Ask him if he can tell you the base or root word. **big** Ask him what happens to the word when you add **-est**. **double the last consonant**

Words like *big* that end with a short vowel and a consonant must double the last consonant before adding **-est**. Ask your student to add **-est** to these words by doubling the last consonant. Ask him to read the base word and the new word aloud.

1) hot **- hottest**   2) fat **- fattest**   3) slim **- slimmest**

c. Tell your student that when we compare the size of two things, we describe one of them as *bigger* than the other. When we compare three or more things we describe one of them as the *biggest*.

Add **-er** and **-est** to these words.

1) fat **- fatter, fattest**   2) tall **- taller, tallest**
3) small **- smaller, smallest**   4) hot **- hotter, hottest**

d. Read the passage with your student.

Parrot drank the warm milk. "Please take the nuts under my pillow," he said.

You have learned that **ar** says /ar/ as in *star*. But when **ar** follows the letter **w**, it usually says **/wor/** as in *warm*. Ask your student to read the words in the Phonics Word Box with you: *war wart warn ward warp*.

Ask him to fill in the blanks with the correct words from the Phonics Word Box.
1) A storm is coming. We must **warn** everyone.
2) Can you get a **wart** from a toad?

e. Help your student number a piece of paper 1 - 4. Dictate the spelling words to your student. If he has any difficulty at all, use the same process used in **2f**.

f. Find page 261 in the *Student Activity Book* and ask your student to copy the sentence on the bottom line and color the page. He may take two days to complete this assignment.

Day 5

a. Ask your student to read "Parrot's Many Troubles" aloud. Celebrate his success and add to his Reading Chart.

b. The story tells us that Parrot's pillow was bumpy because he had nuts under it. Later in the story, Parrot's pillow is unbumpy. Why? **He took the nuts from under the pillow and gave them to Monkey.**

   The word *unbumpy* means **not** bumpy. The prefix **un-** in *unbumpy* means *not*. Ask your student to read these words with you and tell you what they mean.

   1) unhappy - **not happy**   5) unable - **not able**
   2) unhealthy - **not healthy**   6) uncooked - **not cooked**
   3) unfair - **not fair**   7) unlucky - **not lucky**
   4) untidy - **not tidy**   8) unselfish - **not selfish**

c. In Lesson 14, your student learned how to make a naming word mean more than one (plural). For most words, just add an **s**. For words ending in **ch**, **sh**, **s**, or **x**, add **es**. Ex: twig - twigs; bush - bushes

   Ask your student to fill the blank with the plural word.

   1) nut   Parrot began to pick the **nuts**.
   2) wing   He flapped his **wings**.
   3) branch   Monkey swung through the **branches**.
   4) trouble   Parrot had too many **troubles**.
   5) glass   Parrot drank two **glasses** of warm milk.

d. Optional: Spelling test

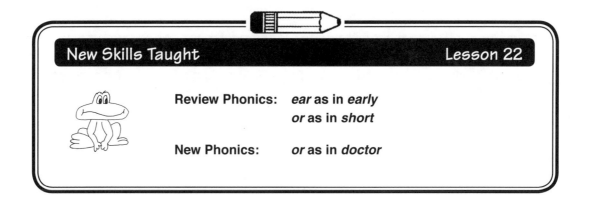

Review Phonics: *ear* as in *early*
                  or as in *short*

New Phonics: *or* as in *doctor*

Day 1

Materials needed:
Up, Down, and Around the Rain Tree

a. Find the story, "Parrot's Green Jacket." Read it to or with your student.

b. Talk to your student about the story. You may use these questions to help you in your discussion.

   1) *What lesson did Parrot learn in the story?* **He learned to share.**
   2) *What did you think about Toucan's situation? Do you know why he was crying?* **He did not have a nice coat to wear to the party.**
   3) *Have you ever had something that somebody else wanted, but you didn't feel you could share it? Tell me about it.*
   4) *Many people are in need right now.* Talk with your student about who is in need of things like food, shelter, clothing, or medicine, and how you feel it is best to help them.

c. In Lesson 21, your student learned that the prefix **un-** means *not*, as in *unhappy*. *Unhappy* means not happy. The story tells us that Parrot unbuttoned his green jacket. The prefix **un-** can also mean to release or undo, as in *unbuttoned*. *Unbuttoned* means to undo the buttons.

   Read these sentences with your student and ask him what the words mean.

   1) *I will* unleash *the dog*. **take the leash off the dog**
   2) *I will* unwrap *the present*. **take the wrapping off the present**
   3) *I will* unscrew *the lid*. **screw off the lid**

d. You have learned that **er, ir,** and **ur** says /**er**/. The letters **ear** also says /**er**/ as in *earn*. Read the words in the Phonics Word Box with your student: *heard pearl earth search.*

Ask him to complete these sentences.

1) Mom has a **pearl** ring.
2) I **heard** a loud noise.
3) I will **search** for the lost coin.
4) The **earth** moves around the sun.

e. Ask your student to copy the spelling words for this week. Read them to or with your student: *learn early heard here.*

Day 2

a. Review the story, "Parrot's Green Jacket," with your students.

b. Talk to your student about Parrot.

1) *How did Parrot feel about his two coats at the beginning of the story?* **He liked them and wanted both of them.**
2) *How did he feel about them during the party?* **He felt warm, itchy, and uncomfortable.**
3) *Why do you think he changed his mind about the two coats?* **He thought about Toucan sitting at home with his old coat while he had two nice coats.**

c. Ask your student to look at the pictures. Ask him to write or dictate phrases about Parrot during these parts of the story.

d. Let's review how to add the suffix **-ed**. To most words, just add **-ed**. To words ending in a silent **e**, drop the **e** before adding **-ed**. Read the passage with your student.

Everyone in the Rain Forest was invited.

Ask your student to look at the word *invited*. Circle the word. *Can you tell me how -ed was added to* invite? **drop the *e* and add *-ed***

Now, read this passage with your student.

Everyone was at the party when Parrot and Monkey arrived.

Ask your student to look at the word *arrived. Can you tell me how -ed was added to* arrive? **drop the e and add -ed**

e. In the two passages in **2d**, the same compound word is used. Circle it. Remember, a compound word is two words joined together to make a new word. Ask your student to tell you the compound word. **everyone** Ask him to draw a line between the two words which make up the compound word. **every / one**

f. How Do You Spell That Word?

Give your student a piece of paper and a pencil. Dictate the spelling words to your student, guiding him through the process.

1) *learn* - The /er/ sound is sometimes spelled **ear**.
2) *here* - This is a common word; help your student as needed.
3) *heard* - Same as 1.
4) *early* - Same as 1.

g. Read the passage with your student.

"Yellow is my favorite color. I think I will let Toucan keep the green jacket."

Your student has learned that **or** says /or/ as in *short*. The letters **or** can also say /er/ as in *doctor*. Ask your student if he can find a word in the first sentence where **or** says /er/. Circle the word. **color**

Read the words in the Phonics Word Box with your student:

doctor actor parlor favor tailor sailor comfort major

Day 3

a. Review the story, "Parrot's Green Jacket."

b. Read the words in the Phonics Word Box with your student: *carried tried cried hurried.*

Ask him to complete these sentences.

1) I hit the ball after I **tried** three times.
2) The baby **cried** for her mother.
3) I **carried** the bags for my mother.
4) We **hurried** to be on time.

c. Context Words: *only favorite nothing*

1) I like red the best. It is my *favorite* color.
2) This is my last candy. It is the *only* one I have now.
3) The empty bag has *nothing* in it.

d. Syllable Sense: **ar/rived re/mem/bered to/ge/ther im/pressed**

e. Ask your student to complete the Spelling Words Puzzle.
   1) heard 2) early 3) here 4) learn

f. Find page 269 in the *Student Activity Book* and ask your student to trace the sentence on the top.

Day 4

a. Review the Word List below for "Parrot's Green Jacket."

color	*only*	*favorite*	*nothing*
Toucan	*arrived*	*remembered*	*unbuttoned*

b. Find the Story Folder in the *Student Activity Book* page 267. Read it to your student, or he may read it to you.

c. Talk to your student about the story. You may use these questions to help you in your discussion.

1) *Tell me the story of "The Little Red Hen" in your own words.* **Self-explanatory**
2) *Why do you think the duck, cat, and dog did not want to help the Little Red Hen?*
   They did not want to work.
3) *Why do you think the duck, cat, and dog wanted to help at the end of the story?*
   They wanted to eat the bread.

d. Ask your student to write or dictate the jobs that Alice Hen did to make the bread. **plant, cut, grind, bake**

e. Read the words in the Phonics Word Box with your student: *warn   wart   war   warp*.

Ask him to complete these sentences.

1) Men fight for their country in a **war**.
2) Noah will **warn** everyone about the flood.
3) The sun may **warp** the plastic.
4) Do you really get a **wart** from a toad?

f. Help your student number a piece of paper 1 - 4. Dictate the spelling words to your student. If he has any difficulty at all, use the same process used in **2f**.

g. Find page 269 in the *Student Activity Book* and ask your student to copy the sentence on the bottom line and color the page. He may take two days to complete this assignment.

Day 5

a. Ask your student to read "Parrot's Green Jacket" aloud. Celebrate his success and add to his Reading Chart.

b. Find page 273 in the *Student Activity Book*. Ask your student to color and cut out the four characters from the story "The Little Red Hen." Using them as finger puppets or stand up characters, ask your student to act out the story, using as many props as he wants to use.

c. Cut the holder off of each character and glue the faces on a separate piece of paper. Ask your student to write or dictate two sentences about each character.

d. This story was written to teach a lesson. Discuss the story and the lesson with your student. Ask him to write or dictate two or three sentences describing the lesson of the story.

e. Optional: Spelling test.

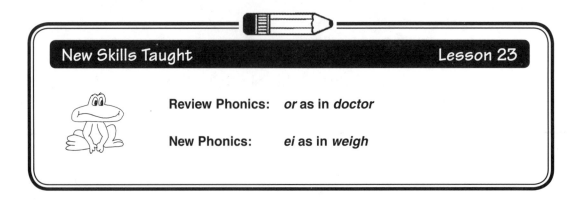

Review Phonics: *or* as in *doctor*

New Phonics: *ei* as in *weigh*

Materials needed:

Up, Down, and Around the Rain Tree

Day 1

a. Find the story, "Puffbird's Nest," in the reader, *Up, Down, and Around the Rain Tree*. Read it to or with your student.

b. Talk to your student about the story. You may use these questions to help you in your discussion.

> 1) *What do you think about the Puffling's behavior?* **The pufflings were a little rowdy.** *What changes in their behavior would have been helpful?* **They could have been more quiet and still.**
>
> 2) *Did Puffbird and the Pufflings show appreciation to Parrot?* **Allow for discussion.**
>
> 3) *How can you show appreciation to people who have helped you?* **Allow for discussion.**

c. Find page 277 in the *Student Activity Book*, and ask your student to cut out the sentence strips for **1c**. Ask him to read the sentences and put them in the order in which they happened.

He may glue the sentence strips in the correct order on one piece of paper. Or, your student may glue one sentence strip on separate pieces of construction paper, adding an illustration on each sheet. They may then be stapled into booklet form.

Ask your student to use the booklet or paper to tell the story from beginning to end.

> 1) **Puffbird's nest was broken by a branch.**
> 2) **Monkey and Parrot came to help Puffbird.**
> 3) **The Pufflings went to Parrot's hole.**
> 4) **The Pufflings jumped and hid.**
> 5) **Puffbird took the Pufflings to their new nest.**

d. Tell your student that a word that shows action, or a doing word, is called a verb. We are going to look at simple verbs.

Ask him to find the word cards for **1d** on page 277 of the *Student Activity Book* and read them to or with him: *look sneeze jump ask cover crash.* Cut out the cards and glue them on the left side of a piece of paper.

Ask your student to make up a sentence using each verb about the story "Puffbird's Nest." He may add an **s**, **es**, or **ed** to the verb, if needed. Ask your student to write or copy the sentence next to the word, and read it aloud to you.

e. Ask your student to read the words in the Phonics Word Box with you: *sailor doctor color actor.*

Ask your student to fill in the blanks with the correct word.
1) Red is my favorite **color**.   2) The **sailor** went on the big ship.
3) Mom is sick. She went to the **doctor**.   4) Ted is an **actor** in the play.

f. Ask your student to copy the spelling words for this week. Read them to or with your student: *color flavor other two.*

Day 2

a. Review the story, "Puffbird's Nest," with your student.

b. Ask your student to look through the reader, *Up, Down, and Around the Rain Tree* and find sound words, such as *Oooooo! Crack! Bang!* Ask him what sound each word means and how it is written in the story.

c. Read the literature passage with your student.

> *"My Pufflings are cold and wet," said Puffbird.*
> *Parrot's hole was warm and dry.*

Ask your student if he notices anything about the words *cold* and *wet*, and *warm* and *dry*. **These are words with opposite meanings, or antonyms.**

d. Read these sentences.

    The Pufflings jumped on Parrot's bed. Up and down. Up and down.

Ask your student to find the pair of antonyms. Circle the words. **up and down**

    The Pufflings crawled under Parrot's bed. In and out. In and out.

Ask your student to find the pair of antonyms. Circle the words. **in and out**

e. How Do You Spell That Word?

Give your student a piece of paper and a pencil. Dictate the spelling words to your student, guiding him through the process.

1) *flavor* - The /**er**/ *sound at the end of a word may be spelled* **or**.
2) *other* - This is a common word; help your student as needed.
3) *color* - Same as 1.
4) *two* - Same as 2.

f. Tell your student that **ei** can say /$\bar{\text{a}}$/ as in *weigh*. Read the words in the Phonics Word Box to your student: *neighbor   weigh   their   veil.*

Ask your student to choose the best word to complete the sentences.

1) They gave us this book. It was **their** book.
2) This is heavy. How much does it **weigh**?
3) He moved next door to me. He is my **neighbor**.

Day 3

a. Review the story, "Puffbird's Nest."

b. Read the passage with your student.

    Parrot and Monkey looked at the nest. "It is truly broken," Parrot said. He tugged at the tree branch.
    "Maybe we can fix it," Monkey said.
    Puffbird shook her head. "Our nest is unfixable."

Ask your student to circle the word *unfixable*. Ask him if he remembers what the prefix **un-** means, as in *unhappy* and *unbuttoned*. **not happy; unfasten the button** Ask him if he can tell you what the word *unfixable* means. **not able to fix**

Read these words with your student and ask him to complete the sentences using one of the words: *unselfish   unimportant   unfriendly*.

1) My grandpa is very kind and **unselfish**.
2) The man looks **unfriendly**, but maybe he's nice.
3) This job is important, but that one is **unimportant**.

c. Context Words: *our   quiet*.

1) We built this treehouse. It is *our* clubhouse. 2) Shh! Please be *quiet*.

d. Syllable Sense: **bro/ken   un/fix/ab/le**

e. Ask your student to complete the Spelling Words Puzzle.

CODE										
a	c	e	f	h	l	o	r	t	v	w
1	2	3	4	5	6	7	8	9	10	11

There are <u>t</u> <u>w</u> <u>o</u> ice cream cones here. The <u>c</u> <u>o</u> <u>l</u> <u>o</u> <u>r</u> of one is green and the
    9 11 7   2 7 6 7 8

<u>o</u> <u>t</u> <u>h</u> <u>e</u> <u>r</u> one is red. Which <u>f</u> <u>l</u> <u>a</u> <u>v</u> <u>o</u> <u>r</u> do you like best?
7 9 5 3 8   4 6 1 10 7 8

f. Find page 283 in the *Student Activity Book* and ask your student to trace the sentence on the top.

Day 4

a. Review the Word List below for "Puffbird's Nest."

their   our   quiet   unfixable   bedcovers   broken

b. Find the Story Folder for "Stag at the Pool" in the *Student Activity Book* page 281. Read it to your student, or he may read it to you.

c. Talk to your student about the story. You may use these questions to help you in your discussion.

    1) *Tell me the story in your own words.* **Self-explanatory**
    2) *Simon was the most handsome deer in the forest. What do you think he liked most about himself?* **his antlers** *Why?* **He thought they were beautiful.**
    3) *What do you think Simon liked the least about himself?* **his legs** *Why?* **He thought they were ugly.**
    4) *How do you think Simon felt about his long, skinny legs at the end of the story?* **He was thankful for them.**

d. Read the passage with your student.

    She covered her Pufflings with her wings.

Ask your student if Puffbird was covering one or more than one Puffling with her wings. **more than one Puffling** How do you know? *Pufflings* **has an *s* at the end, meaning more than one.**

Ask your student if Puffbird was covering her Pufflings with one or more than one wing. **more than one wing** How do you know? *Wings* **has an *s* at the end, meaning more than one.**

Review with your student that to make a word mean more than one, or plural, you usually just add an **s**. To make a word ending in **ch, sh, s,** and **x** mean more than one, add **es**. Ask your student to write the plural form of these words in the blanks.

    1) dog   We saw three **dogs** at the beach.
    2) branch   Many **branches** fell down.
    3) ax   My dad has two **axes** in the shed.
    4) sign   There are two **signs** near our road.
    5) ash   I swept the **ashes**.

e. Help your student number a piece of paper 1 - 4. Dictate the spelling words to your student. If he has any difficulty at all, use the same process used in **2e**.

f. Find page 283 in the *Student Activity Book* and ask your student to copy the sentence on the bottom line and color the page. He may take two days to complete this assignment.

Day 5

a. Ask your student to read "Puffbird's Nest" aloud. Celebrate his success and add to his Reading Chart.

b. Read the passage with your student.

> *Parrot's hole was warm and dry. The Pufflings stopped sneezing. But now they jumped on Parrot's bed.*

Whose hole was warm and dry? **Parrot's** *Whose bed did the Pufflings jump on?* **Parrot's** *Circle the word* Parrot's. *Why is the word* Parrot's *written with an apostrophe and s?* **to show possession or ownership**

Ask your student to write his name in the blank to show that he owns each item listed.
1) **Possible answer: John's** bike
2) **Possible answer: Haley's** toy
3) **Possible answer: Leo's** coat

Teacher's Note: If your student's name ends with an *s*, just add an apostrophe. Explain to your student that his name is special, and there is a special rule for names ending in *s*. He will learn this in a higher level book.

c. Optional: Spelling test

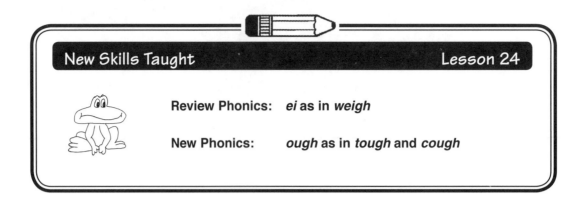

Review Phonics: *ei* as in *weigh*

New Phonics: *ough* as in *tough* and *cough*

Materials needed:

Up, Down, and Around the Rain Tree

Day 1

a. Find the story, "Monkey's Blue Umbrella," in the reader, *Up, Down, and Around the Rain Tree*. Read it to or with your student.

b. Talk to your student about the story. You may use these questions to help you in your discussion.

    1) *Monkey was prepared for rain even though it did not look like rain. How did Monkey's preparation help his friends?* **They stayed mostly dry.**

    2) *Every time someone new came along, everyone had to give up a little more space. Did Monkey think there was enough room for everyone under his umbrella?* **Not at first, but after, he realized there was more room than he imagined.**

    3) Read Matthew 7:12 to your student. *This Scripture is often called the "Golden Rule." Why do you think it is called the Golden Rule?* **Allow for discussion.**

    4) *Tell me a situation in which you could practice the Golden Rule.* **Answers will vary.**

c. Read this passage to or with your student.

> *"We don't need your umbrella," Parrot said. "The sun is shining."*

Ask your student to circle the word, *shining*, and copy it. Tell him the word and ask him what letters were added to the base or main part of the word. **-ing** Tell him to cross out the **-ing**. Show him the word *shine*. Ask him to tell you how **-ing** was added to the word. **Drop the silent e and add -ing.**

Ask your student to add **-ing** to these words ending with a silent **e.**

1) share - **sharing**   2) close - **closing**
3) make - **making**   4) shine - **shining**

d. Read the words in the Phonics Word Box with your student: *their neighbor weigh veil.*

Ask your student to look at the picture, read the sentences and put an X next to the sentence that best describes the picture.

___ 1) How much does she weigh?
X 2) She is my new neighbor.
___ 3) Their dog is nice.
___ 4) Do you have a veil?

Write a sentence about the picture using a word that ends in **-ing**.

e. Ask your student to copy the spelling words for this week. Read them to or with your student: *their weigh from for.*

Day 2

a. Review the story, "Monkey's Blue Umbrella," with your student.

b. Ask your student to list the four characters who shared the umbrella. List them in the order they came under it, using the words *first, second, etc..* **First came Monkey. Second came Parrot. Third came Sloth. Fourth came Toucan.**

c. Read this passage to or with your student.

Sloth was bigger than Parrot.
She was bigger than Monkey himself.

Ask your student to look at the pictures, read the words, and fill in the blanks with the best word: *bigger biggest.*

1) Monkey is **bigger** than Parrot.   2) Sloth is the **biggest** of them all.

Ask your student to look at the pictures. Read these words to or with your student and ask him to fill in the blanks correctly: *taller tallest shorter shortest*.

3) The house is **taller** than the tree.
4) The pole is the **tallest** of all them.

5) The dog is **smaller** than the boy.
6) The bird is the **smallest** of them all.

d. Ask your student to look at this word: *don't*. Tell him that this word is a shortened way of saying *do not*. Show him the words *do not*, and ask him to copy the words.

Tell him that the apostrophe takes the place of the missing letter. Ask him to cross out the missing letter. **do n̶o̶t̶** Ask him to write the word *don't* beside *do not*.

Continue the same process with these contractions: isn't - **is n̶o̶t̶**; can't - **can n̶o̶t̶**

e. How Do You Spell That Word?

Give your student a piece of paper and a pencil. Dictate the spelling words to your student, helping him learn spelling rules.

1) *their - The /ā/ sound in the middle of a word may be spelled ei.*
2) *weigh - Same as 1.*
3) *from - This is a common word; help your student as needed.*
4) *for - Same as 3.*

f. Tell your student that **ough** says /uff/ as in *rough* or /off/ as in *cough*. Read the words in the Phonics Word Box with your student: *rough tough enough cough*.

Ask him to read each sentence and put an X beside the sentence which best describes the picture.
_____ 1) Jim is a tough, little boy.
__X__ 2) Sally had a cough. She went to bed.
_____ 3) She had enough candy for one day.
_____ 4) Dad sanded the rough wood.

 g. Write a sentence about the picture using a contraction.

Day 3

a. Review the story, "Monkey's Blue Umbrella," with your student.

b. Ask your student to tell you the story in his own words.

c. Ask your student to fold three pieces of paper in half widthwise. Cut them on the fold line and staple them together on the side. Ask him to write the story title, "Monkey's Blue Umbrella," on the front.

Find page 295 in the *Student Activity Book*, and ask him to cut out the sentence strips for **3c**. Ask him to put the cards in the correct order. Glue one card on each page and illustrate them.

d. Read the passage with your student.

> *"Oh, dear! Oh, dear! I am getting wet!" said Sloth.*

Ask your student to circle the exclamation marks. *Why do the sentences end with an exclamation mark?* **to show strong feeling** Ask your student to read the words with feeling, expressing how he thinks Sloth would have said it.

e. Read the passage with your student.

> *"May I share your umbrella?" Sloth asked.*

Ask your student to circle the question mark. *Why does the quote end with a question mark?* **It is an asking sentence.** Ask your student to read the words, expressing how he thinks Sloth would have said it.

f. Context Words: *umbrella ruined beginning imagined.*

1) It is raining. I will take my *umbrella*.
2) I fell in the dirt. My new shirt is *ruined*.
3) She made up a story. She *imagined* the whole scene.
4) We must start at the *beginning*.

g. Ask your student to complete the Spelling Words Puzzle.
   1) **weigh**   3) **from**
   2) **for**   4) **their**

h. Find page 291 in the *Student Activity Book* and ask your student to trace the sentence on the top.

Day 4

a. Review the Word List below for "Monkey's Blue Umbrella."

enough   umbrella   ruined   beginning   imagined   sunshine

b. Read the Story Folder, "The Fox Who Lost His Tail," on page 293 of the *Student Activity Book* to your student, or he may read it to you.

c. Talk to your student about the story. You may use these questions to help you in your discussion.

   1) *Tell me the story in your own words.*
   2) *If you were the little fox, would you have taken the short cut path? Why or why not?*
   3) *Why do you think he took that path?* **He was late for a meeting; he was stubborn.**
   4) *Why did the fox want everyone to look like him with no hair on his tail?* **Then he wouldn't feel so badly about losing his bushy tail.**

d. Tell your student that you can often recognize an animal by its tail. Find page 295 in the *Student Activity Book* and cut out the pictures. Cut out the pictures of the tails and glue them on the matching animal.

   Ask him to copy the correct word under each animal: *fox   beaver   rabbit.*

e. Read the passage with your student.

   Sloth was bigger than Parrot.

   Tell your student that Parrot was big, but Sloth was bigger. When we compare two things or people, we usually use **-er.** Ask your student to complete these sentences. Ex: Parrot was big. Sloth was bigger than Parrot.

   1) Monkey was wet. Parrot was **wetter** than Monkey.
   2) Toucan was clean. Monkey was **cleaner** than Toucan.
   3) Monkey was small. Toucan was **smaller** than Monkey.

f. Help your student number a piece of paper 1 - 4. Dictate the spelling words to your student. If he has any difficulty at all, use the same process used in **2e**.

g. Find page 291 in the *Student Activity Book* and ask your student to copy the sentence on the bottom line and color the page. He may take two days to complete this assignment.

Day 5

5. a. Ask your student to read "Monkey's Blue Umbrella" aloud. Celebrate his success and add to his Reading Chart.

    b. Review with your student that two words joined together to make a new word is called a compound word.

    Ask your student to look at the following words and make four compound words using the word *sun* at the beginning of each word: shine flower set light **sunshine sunflower sunset sunlight**

    Write two of the words on a separate piece of paper and illustrate the words.

    c. Read the passage with your student.

    All at once the rain stopped. Sloth stepped into the sunshine.

    Ask your student to underline the words *stopped* and *stepped*. Ask your student to circle the base word of each word. **stop, step** Ask him what suffix was added to each word. **-ed** Ask him to tell you the rule for adding **ed** to words ending with a single, short vowel and consonant. **When adding the suffix -ed to a word ending with a single, short vowel and a consonant, double the last consonant before adding -ed.**

    Ask your student to complete the sentences by adding **-ed** to the words. Ask him to read the sentences to you. Give your student any help he may need.

    1) The bunny **hopped** into the hole.
    2) I **patted** the dog.
    3) The bubbles **popped**.

    d. Optional: Spelling test

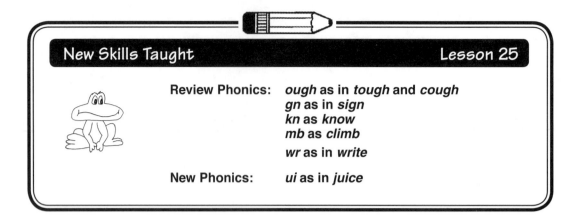

Review Phonics: *ough* as in *tough* and *cough*
      gn as in *sign*
      kn as *know*
      mb as *climb*
      wr as in *write*

New Phonics: *ui* as in *juice*

Materials needed:

Up, Down, and Around the Rain Tree

craft materials

Day 1

a. Find the story, "Sweet Figgy Cream Pie," in the reader, *Up, Down, and Around the Rain Tree*. Read it to or with your student.

b. Talk to your student about the story. You may use these questions to help you in your discussion.

1) *What did Parrot think of Monkey picking figs for everyone else?* **He thought Monkey was foolish.**
2) *Do you think that is what Parrot would have done?*
3) *Do you think Monkey did the right thing?*
4) *What were Monkey's rewards for helping others?* **He received figgy juice and figgy cream pie.**

c. Read the words in the Phonics Word Box with your student: *tough enough rough cough*.

Ask him to choose one of the words to complete these sentences.

1) I drank **enough** water.
2) The race was **tough**, but I finished.
3) Sandpaper feels **rough**.
4) The baby is sick and has a bad **cough**.

d. Ask your student to copy the spelling words for this week. Read them to or with your student: *rough tough should was*.

Day 2

    a. Review the story, "Sweet Figgy Cream Pie," with your student.

    b. Talk to your student about Monkey. Review all the stories and find the parts that include Monkey. Discuss what kind of a character Monkey is in this book.

    c. Ask your student to write or dictate phrases about Monkey. Ask him to include his opinions, too.

    d. Read these sentences with your student. Remind your student that a doing word, or verb, shows action. Ask him to circle the verbs in each sentence, and act them out.

        1) Sloth (**jumped**) onto a fig vine.

        2) Monkey (**climbed**) the fig vines.

        3) Parrot (**licked**) his beak.

    e. How Do You Spell That Word?

      Give your student a piece of paper and a pencil. Dictate the spelling words to your student, helping him learn spelling rules.

        1) *tough* - *The /**uff**/ sound may be spelled* **ough**.
        2) *should* - This is a common word; help your student as needed.
        3) *rough* - Same as 1.
        4) *was* - Same as 2.

    f. Tell your student that **ui** says **/oo/** as in *juice*. Read the words in the Phonics Word Box with your student: *juice suit fruit*.

      Ask him to complete the sentences choosing the best word.

        1) I like to drink orange **juice**.
        2) Apple is my favorite **fruit**.
        3) My dad wears a **suit** to work.

Day 3

    a. Review the story, "Sweet Figgy Cream Pie," with your student.

b. Ask your student to scan through the story and find the compound words. Remind him that a compound word is two words joined together to make a new word, such as *everything*.

page 49-cannot　　　　　　　　　　**page 55-puffbird, something**
page 52-puffbird　　　　　　　　　　**page 56-something**
page 53-puffbird

c. Review with your student that a contraction is a shortened way of joining two words joined together with an apostrophe such as *don't* or *do not*. Ask your student to copy the word *what's*. Tell him that *what's* is a contraction for *what is* or *what has*. Beside the word, ask him to copy the words, *what is* and *what has*. Ask him to cross out the letter(s) for which the apostrophe takes the place. **cross out the letter i in** *what is*, **cross out the letters ha in** *what has* Continue the same process with these contractions.

1) that's - that is or that has　　　　**3) he's - he is or he has**
2) it's - it is or it has　　　　　　　**4) she's - she is or she has**

d. Remind your student that sometimes a letter in a word is silent, such as in *know*, where the **k** makes no sound. Read these words to or with your student and ask him to cross out the silent letter in each one. Ex: know

　　1) sign　　　　4) write
　　2) knot　　　　5) lamb
　　3) climb　　　　6) gnat

e. Ask your student to complete the Spelling Words Puzzle.

　　Ex:　　　the + here - he = there
　　1) shout + told - tot = **should**
　　2) row + tough - tow = **rough**
　　3) tough + was - saw = **tough**
　　4) wrap + a + snip - nip - rap = **was**

f. Find page 301 in the *Student Activity Book* and ask your student to trace the sentence on the top.

Day 4

a. Review the Word List below for "Sweet Figgy Cream Pie."

　juice　　*careful*　　*almost*　　*basket*　　*climbed*　　*figgy*

174

b. Look through the reader, *Up, Down, and Around the Rain Tree* with your student. Talk about the characters, stories, and setting. You may use these questions to help you in your discussion.

1) *Tell me one of the stories in your own words.*
2) *Choose a character and tell me what you remember about him/her.*
3) *Can you find the Table of Contents, title page, and copyright page?*
4) *Who wrote the story? Who drew the pictures?*

c. Read the passage with your student.

> *"Be careful!" Monkey shouted.*

Ask your student to circle the word *careful*. Tell him the word means *to be full of care*. The suffix **-ful** means to be *full of*. Read these words with your student and ask him to tell you what he thinks they mean.

1) beautiful - **full of beauty**
2) thankful - **full of thanks**
3) helpful - **full of help**

d. Find page 305 in the *Student Activity Book*. Ask your student to use the pictures to create a Rain Tree project of his choice. He will have time tomorrow to complete the project.

1) Color and cut out the pictures. Use a box to create a 3-D scene, or diorama, of the Rain Tree. Your student may write or dictate a summary of a few stories or make up his own.

2) Color and cut out the pictures, glue each picture on a piece of blank paper, and ask your student to write or dictate a sentence for each one.

3) Create a new story about the characters. Staple several pages together. Write the story in the book and glue the pictures as desired. Color the pictures. Title your story.

e. Help your student number a piece of paper 1 - 4. Dictate the spelling words to your student. If he has any difficulty at all, use the same process used in **2e**.

f. Find page 301 in the *Student Activity Book* and ask your student to copy the sentence on the bottom line and color the page. He may take two days to complete this assignment.

Day 5

5. a. Ask your student to read "Sweet Figgy Cream Pie" aloud. Celebrate his success and add to his Reading Chart. He has now completed *Up, Down, and Around the Rain Tree*.
Have him add the book cover to his Reading Chart.

b. Continue work on the Rain Tree project.

c. Present the project to a small group.

d. Optional: Spelling test

e. Today, complete *Assessment 5* with your student.

Assessment 5
(Lessons 21 - 25)

Assessment 5 is a written assessment. Find page 302 in his *Student Activity Book*. Ask him to complete it as you instruct him.

1. *Add **y** to the end of these words.*

   a. *rain* **rainy**
   b. *leak* **leaky**
   c. *smell* **smelly**

2. *Drop the silent **e** and add **y** to the end of these words.*

   a. *shake* **shaky**
   b. *rose* **rosy**
   c. *slime* **slimy**

3. *Drop the **y** and add **ies** to these words.*

   a. *candy* **candies**
   b. *baby* **babies**
   c. *pony* **ponies**

4. *Make compound words using the words from both columns.*

   a. **eyelash**
   b. **highway**
   c. **waterfall**

5. *An action word is called a verb. Underline the verbs in these sentences.*

   a. Jordan **grinned** from ear to ear.
   b. Tom **hit** the ball.
   c. Jesse **slept** in his bed.

6. *Cross out the letters to make a contraction. Write the contraction.*

   a. did nøt **didn't**
   b. I h̸ave **I've**
   c. we a̸re **we're**

7. *Add **-ful** to the end of these words.*

    a. cup - **cupful**
    b. hand - **handful**
    c. thank - **thankful**

8. *Add **un-** to the beginning of these words.*

    a. screw - **unscrew**
    b. cover - **uncover**
    c. able - **unable**

9. *Choose the correct word.*

    a. John is **taller** than Mike.
    b. Tommy is the **tallest** of all the boys.

10. *Add **-er** and **-est** to these words.*

    a. thin **thinner**   **thinnest**
    b. dim **dimmer**   **dimmest**

Introduction to Part 3

These final eleven lessons provide your student with the transition needed for third grade work. The format of the lessons have changed to be like those in *Learning Language Arts Through Literature, The Yellow Book*. Explain to your student why there is a change in the look of the lesson and use that as an opportunity to praise his accomplishments.

The lessons are written directly to the student. If he is not ready to make this transition, continue with your student. Each lesson begins by your student copying a literature passage. This is the time to help him with any difficulty he may have in letter formations. The lesson ends with your student writing the same passage. This is the time for him to use his best handwriting.

Focus on Spelling is provided for each lesson. Puzzles are still given to review the words, but your student will now learn how to spell the words on his own using the See-Spell-Say method. The student is to: 1. Look and *see* the spelling word. 2. *Spell* the word. 3. *Say* the word.

In Part 3 the literature passages provide a basis for grammar and writing skills. Many of these activities include writing assignments. If your student has difficulty with composing and writing sentences, give all the help needed, even if you write the sentences for him. The first step to writing is thinking and organizing thoughts. Use this time to strengthen those skills, and the writing will come eventually.

Two *Successful Reading Series* readers are used in this section for phonics instruction, writing, and thinking skills. Use the readers and phonics instruction as your student needs them.

Successful Reading Series for Part 3

Underwater Friends
Famous People

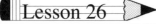

Harry was a white dog with black spots. On his birthday, he got a present from Grandma. It was a woolen sweater with roses on it.

No Roses for Harry! by Gene Zion
Text copyright © 1958 by Eugene Zion
Reprinted by permission of HarperCollins Publishers

Materials needed:
Underwater Friends

1. a. Listen as your teacher reads the literature passage. Copy the sentences. Compare your copy to the model and make corrections.

   b. It is fun to visit relatives. Tell your teacher the meaning of the word *relative*. Who are your relatives? Write down the names of some of your relatives.

   c. Using an atlas or map, find the location of a special relative not living in your town. Talk to your teacher about his town and how long it would take to get there. Special people are worth making effort for, whether it's in the form of a visit, phone call, or letter.

   d. Make a card or draw a picture for a relative or a friend and send it today.

   e. Copy the spelling words from Focus on Spelling:
   white   black   roses   spots
   Bonus Word: *along*

2.
a. Harry - white dog with black spots

woolen sweater

2. a. Reread the literature passage. Underline the words that tell the color of Harry, and underline the word that tells what kind of sweater he got from Grandma. A word that describes something is called an **adjective**. Adjectives tell either what kind, which one, or how many.

Grammar Guide
Adjective - a word that describes a naming word, or noun

180

b. Look around the room and find five things that you can better tell about by using a describing word, or an adjective.
Ex: clean desk, red book, happy child

Write or dictate a sentence for each of the things, using the adjective in the sentence.
Ex: I have a clean desk.

c. Pretend you are a detective and listen to the conversations of your family and friends. Make a list of five adjectives that they use in their descriptions of people, places, or things.

d. See-Spell-Say
Look and **see** each word in the spelling list. **Spell** each word aloud. **Say** the word.

3. a. In the literature passage there are several words that have the letter **s** in them. All of these words do not have the same /s/ sound. Some have an **s** that says /z/ as in *has*. Circle the words with **s** saying **z**.

b. Read each word and indicate if the **s** makes a /s/ or /z/ sound: *spot sat pass was sweater has rose present*

c. A noun is a naming word. Many times we add an **s** to the end of the noun to mean more than one. Read the words on page 308 in the *Student Activity Book* and write the word with an **s** at the end, next to each word.

Read the new words and, orally, make up a sentence with each word.

d. Spelling Words Puzzle

4. a. Find the story, "A Surprise Party," in the reader, *Underwater Friends*, and read it to your teacher.

b. Discuss the story with your teacher:
1) *Tell me the story in your own words.*
2) *If you were Seahorse, how would you have felt after Lobster's phone call? Why?*
3) *What advice would you give Octopus and Seahorse about Tuna's party?*

3.
a. was, his, present, roses

✎ Teacher's Note: For this activity, please provide index cards with *s* and *z* written on them for the student to indicate the kind of *s* sound in the word.

b. spot - /s/
   sat - /s/
   pass - /s/
   was - /z/
   sweater - /s/
   has - /z/
   rose - /z/
   present - /z/

c. 1) roses
   2) spots
   3) cats
   4) bags
   5) books

d. 1) roses
   2) spots
   3) black
   4) white

✐ **Teacher's Note: Keep it simple. This is only a simple introduction to researching a topic.**
4.
c. the L volume

d. who -h
   whose - h
   whom - h
   where - w
   whole - h
   why - w
   when - w

4) *If you were Tuna, how would you have felt when you read the sign?*

c. Discuss the character of Lobster with your teacher. Although we know very little about him so far, what is your impression of him? Which letter volume of the encyclopedia would we look at to find information on lobsters? Look up *lobster* in the encyclopedia or other reference book. Find a few facts about them. List those facts.

d. The letter combination **ph** makes an **/f/** sound. This letter combination can be found at the beginning, middle, or end of a word. Read the words in the Phonics Word Box with your teacher: *graph   phone   phase   dolphin   phonics.*

The letter combination **wh** makes two different sounds: **/w/** and **/h/**. This letter combination is found at the beginning of a word. Read these words and decide what sound the **wh** makes in each word: *who   whose   whom   where   whole   why   when.*

e. Birthdays are special days. If you have pictures of your birthdays, share them with a group and tell a story.

Answer these questions about your birthdays.

1) *What special people did you have at your birthday party?*
2) *What special activities did you do at your birthday party?*
3) *What special things did you have at your birthday party?*
4) *What special feelings did you feel at your birthday party?*

f. Draw a picture of your favorite birthday and write or dictate three to four sentences describing the events of that day.

g. Review your spelling words orally.

5. a. Review any words from the story that you have had difficulty reading.

b. Read the story, "A Surprise Party," aloud. Then mark the Reading Chart for that story.

c. In the story, Tuna reacted in the opposite way than what Seahorse and Octopus expected. Antonyms are words with opposite meanings. The antonym of *hot* is *cold*. Listen to your teacher as she reads a word. Look at the words listed in your *Student Activity Book* to find a word that is an antonym of each word she reads.

out	first	frowned	bad
goodbye	hate	up	sad
early	hot	wrong	no

d. Using a pair of antonyms from above, write sentences with each word that shows the opposite meanings.
Ex: I climbed *up* the hill. I slid *down* the hill.

Do this with two other pairs of antonyms.

e. Make a card out of construction paper for a friend or relative. It can be a birthday card or *I'm thinking of you* card. Decorate the card, write a message inside, and mail it.

f. Copy the literature passage using your best handwriting.

g. Optional: Spelling test

5.
c. out - in
  goodbye - hello
  early - late
  first - last
  hate - love
  hot - cold
  frowned - smiled
  up - down
  wrong - right
  bad - good
  sad - happy
  no - yes

When he tried it on, he felt cosy and snug. But he still didn't like the roses.

No Roses for Harry! by Gene Zion
Text copyright © 1958 by Eugene Zion
Reprinted by permission of HarperCollins Publishers

✏ **Teacher's Note:** The word *cosy* in the literature passage may also be spelled *cozy*.

Materials needed:
Underwater Friends

✏ **Teacher's Note:** If you can, give your student an example of what you did when you had mixed feelings about something.

✏ **Teacher's Note:** Your student will dictate or write sentences on the bottom part of the paper in 2c.

1. a. Listen as your teacher reads the literature passage. Copy the sentences. Compare your copy to the model and make corrections.

   b. Discuss the literature passage with your teacher:

      1) *Harry seems to be struggling. He has different feelings about the sweater.*
      2) *What good feelings does he have about the sweater?*
      3) *What bad feeling does he have?*
      4) *Have you ever had both good and bad feelings about something? Tell me about it. What did you do?*
      5) *What do you think Harry will do?*
      6) *A good way to understand your feelings and what to do about them is to talk with your parents.*

   c. You have read several things about Harry the dog. Reread the sentences in this lesson and the last lesson. Fold a piece of paper in half width-wise. Draw a picture of Harry with his birthday gift, showing how Harry feels on the top part of the paper.

   d. Copy the spelling words from Focus on Spelling:
      people   they   when   saw

2. a. When we change a word from something that is happening right now, to something that has already happened, we change the spelling of the word.

      Ex: walk - walked, play - played,
           look - looked, jump - jumped

When the word we are changing ends with a consonant and **y**, we have to do something different. We have to change the **y** to an **i** and then add **-ed**.
Ex: cry - cried, spy - spied

Underline the word in our literature passage that follows this pattern.

b. Change these words to show that they have already happened. Use the new words you made in a sentence. This activity can be done orally or in writing. *try fry dry*

c. Discuss with your teacher how you would feel if you were in the same situation as Harry. On the picture you drew for **1c**, write or dictate two sentences that tell how you would feel if you were Harry.

d. See-Spell-Say
Look and **see** each word in the spelling list. **Spell** each word aloud. **Say** the word.

3. a. Think about some books you have read. List five of your favorite books. Ask your teacher for help if you need it.

b. What are the names of the most important characters in your favorite stories? Why did you enjoy these books? Ask your teacher for help if you need it.

Give an oral report by reading these sentences aloud.

c. Spelling Words Puzzle

4. a. Find the story, "A New Friend," in the reader, *Underwater Friends*, and read it to your teacher.

4.
b. 1) Self-explanatory
2) because she looked different; Answers will vary.
3) Allow for discussion.
4) Allow for discussion.
5) Answers will vary.

4.
d. 1) different
2) knew
3) to know

e. weak / week
not strong / 7 days

see / sea - look at something / ocean

heel / heal - the back part of your foot / to cure

meet / meat - greet someone / food you eat

real / reel - not pretend / a fishing reel

beat / beet - to hit / a red vegetable

---

b. Discuss the story with your teacher:

1) *Tell me the story in your own words.*
2) *Why were Octopus and Tuna so curious about Clownfish? How do you think you would have felt if you saw Clownfish?*
3) *Do you think Octopus and Tuna like Clownfish? Why or why not?*
4) *How would you describe Clownfish? Do you think she will make a good friend? Why?*
5) *How are you and your friends alike and how are you different?*

c. You have learned that **ea** usually says /ē/ as in *dear* Sometimes **ea** in the middle of a word says /ā/ as in *bear*. Read the words in the Phonics Word Box to your teacher: *great bear pear break wear steak tear.*

d. Read the first sentence in the story. Discuss it with your teacher:

1) *What does the word* new *mean in this sentence?*
2) *Do you know another word that sounds the same as* new *but is spelled differently and has a different meaning?*
3) *Do you know what* knew *means?*
4) New *and* knew *are called homonyms. Homonyms are words that usually sound the same but have different meanings and can be spelled differently.*

e. Read the words and draw lines to the matching homonyms. Tell your teacher what each word means.

weak	heal
see	reel
heel	week
meet	beet
real	meet
beat	sea

f. Using a word pair from **4e**, write a sentence for each word so the meaning of the word is clear.

Read the sentences to your teacher. Do this with two or three pairs of homonyms.

Ex: I cut my *heel* on the glass. I hope my cut will *heal* soon.

g. Review your spelling words orally.

5. a. Review any words from the story that you have had difficulty reading.

b. Read the story, "A New Friend," aloud. Then mark the Reading Chart for that story.

c. Find the table of contents in *Underwater Friends*. On what page does the story, "A New Friend," begin? Turn to the page where the story begins.

Listen to your teacher as she reads a word and uses it in a sentence. Look at the page of the story indicated to find a word that is a homonym of that word and make up a sentence with that homonym in it.

(p. 9) sea - The characters in our story live in the sea.
(p. 10) knot - I tied a knot *in my shoelace.*
(p. 10) high - The hill is too high *to climb.*
(p. 11) meat - We had meat *and potatoes for dinner.*
(p. 13) write - Will you write *a letter for me?*
(p. 13) hole - There is a hole *in my sock.*
(p. 14) hear - Did you hear *me call you?*

5.
c. page 9

5.
c. see - I see the dog.
 not - He does not like yogurt.
 hi - Please tell Granny I said "hi."
 meet - Did you meet Bill yet?
 right - Is that answer right?
 whole - I ate a whole apple for lunch.
 here - Come here, little dog.

d. the C volume

d. To look up *clownfish* in an encyclopedia, in which letter volume would we look?
Optional: Look up clownfish in the encyclopedia or other reference book.

On a separate piece of paper list several facts about this animal. With your teacher's help, write a sentence about each fact and draw a picture of the fish.

e. Copy the literature passage using your best handwriting.

f. Optional: Spelling test

When people saw it, they laughed.
When dogs saw it, they barked. Harry
made up his mind then and there to lose
Grandma's present.

No Roses for Harry! by Gene Zion
Text copyright © 1958 by Eugene Zion
Reprinted by permission of HarperCollins Publishers

Materials needed:
Harry the Dirty Dog
by Gene Zion

Underwater Friends

✐ **Teacher's Note:**
Remind your student
that this week's
literature passage is
a continuation of the
story about Harry and
the sweater.

1. a. Listen as your teacher reads the literature passage. Copy the sentences. Compare your copy to the model and make corrections.

   b. Discuss the literature passage with your teacher:

      1) *Harry is having a very hard time with his feelings about his present from Grandma. Something happened to Harry that made him feel very bad.*
      2) *Can you find and read the lines that tell what happened to Harry?*
      3) *When people and dogs made fun of Harry, he decided to "lose" the present. Do you think Harry is doing the right thing? Why or why not?*

   c. Write or dictate two to three sentences telling what you think about Harry's gift and his decision to "lose" it.

   d. Copy the spelling words from Focus on Spelling:
      bark   mind   made   some

2. a. There are four words in our sentences that take the place of a noun. A word that takes place of a noun is called a **pronoun**. Underline the pronouns in our sentences, and tell your teacher the name of the person, place, or thing they replace.

2.
a. it - sweater or
   Grandma's present

   they - people

   it - sweater or
   Grandma's present

   they - dogs

   his - Harry

✐ **Teacher's Note:**
The pronoun *they* **is**
used twice, replacing
a different noun each
time.

Grammar Guide
Pronoun - a word that takes the place of a noun

189

b. Here is a list of common pronouns:

Pronoun Box			
I	me	you	she
we	they	it	he

Choose a story that you have read with your teacher. See if you can find at least five pronouns in the story. Tell your teacher the name of the person, place, or thing they replace.

I   *replaces your name*
we   *replaces you and another person*
it   *replaces an object*
she *replaces one girl or woman*
you *replaces someone who is being referred to; male or female; singular or plural*
they *replaces two people who are being referred to*
he   *replaces one boy or man*

Find page 323 in the *Student Activity Book* and cut out the pronoun word cards for **2b**. Read the top half of the sentence strips. Fill in the blanks correctly in the sentence strips that follow.

Cut out the sentence strips, match them, and glue the correct pronoun in each blank.

c. See-Spell-Say
Look and **see** each word in the spelling list. **Spell** each word aloud. **Say** the word.

✏ **Teacher's Note: Keep it simple by addressing the envelope for your student.**

d. It is thoughtful to thank people for things they do for us, or give us. Think of someone you can write a thank you note to, even Dad or Grandma. Look at the parts of a letter: date on upper right, greeting, body, closing and signature. Here is an example:

> June 10, 1998 *(date)*
>
> Dear Grandma, *(greeting)*
>
>   Thank you very much for the book and toy. I like them very much. Tigers are my favorite. *(body)*
>
> Love, *(closing)*
> Bobby *(signature)*

3. a. Read the book, *Harry the Dirty Dog*, by Gene Zion to or with your teacher. Discuss the illustrations with your teacher, looking for detail and expression.

   b. What is Harry's goal in the beginning of the book?

      1) *Do you think Harry achieved his goal?*
      2) *Have you ever wanted to get very dirty or not take a bath?*
      3) *Do you think all children or pets feel like this at some time?*
      4) *Have you or your family ever had a special time of fun playing in the dirt?*

      Draw a picture of you and your family having a fun time, possibly building sand castles or making mud pies!

   c. Find the two pictures of a dog on page 319 of the *Student Activity Book*. Color one dog to look dirty like Harry, black with white spots; color the other dog to look clean, whitewith black spots. Write words that describe each dog on the lines below each picture.

      Suggested words to use to describe the dogs are: clean, fluffy, muddy, filthy, etc. With your teacher's help, use a thesaurus and read the synonyms for *clean* and *dirty*.

   d. Spelling Words Puzzle

4. a. Find the story, "A New Bike for Lobster," and read it to your teacher.

   b. Discuss the story with your teacher:

      1) *Tell me the story in your words.*
      2) *Why did Lobster think he would have his new bike tomorrow?*
      3) *Why was he not able to buy his new bike?*
      4) *If you were Lobster, how would you feel now? What would you do now?*
      5) *There is an old saying: "Don't count your chickens before they hatch." What do you think that means?*
      6) *How do you think this phrase applies to Lobster?*

3.
d. 1) bark
   2) some
   3) mind
   4) made

4.
b. 1) Answers will vary.
   2) He thought he could sell plenty of things and have the money right away.
   3) He did not sell anything and had no money.
   4) Allow time for discussion.
   5) Don't count on something until you have it.
   6) He should not count on having his bike until he has the money.

c. Make a list of ways that you could get the money to buy a new toy if you really wanted one.

d. The letters **er**, **ir**, **ur** says /er/. Sometimes when a word ends with **or** it says /er/ as in *doctor*. Also, sometimes when a word ends with **ar** it says /er/ as in *dollar*. Read the words in the Phonics Word Box to your teacher: *dollar collar actor parlor error major cellar*.

e. Read these words to your teacher: *little small*. These words have similar meanings. Words that have similar meanings are called synonyms. Tell your teacher a synonym for each of the following words: *big pretty cold hug mix cry*

f. Review your spelling words orally.

5. a. Review any words from the story, "A Bike for Lobster," that you have had difficulty reading.

b. Read the story aloud. Then mark the Reading Chart for that story.

c. Find the table of contents in your reader. Find the beginning of "A New Bike for Lobster."

Remember, synonyms are words of similar meaning, such as *small* and *little*. Listen to your teacher as she reads a word. Look at the page of the story indicated to find a word that is a synonym for that word.

greatest (p. 17)   *aged/antique (p. 18)*   *cash (p. 20)*
fine (p. 17)   *purchase (p. 20)*   *pay out (p. 22)*
large (p. 17, 18)

d. Copy the literature passage using your best handwriting.

e. Optional: Spelling test

4.
e. *big* - large, huge
pretty - beautiful, lovely
cold - cool, chilly
hug - squeeze, embrace
mix - stir, blend
cry - weep, sob

5.
c. *greatest* - best
fine - nice
large - big
aged/antique - old
purchase - buy
cash - money
pay out - spend

First he tried to lose it in the pet department, but a man found it and gave it back. Then he tried to lose it in the grocery department, but a lady found it and gave it back.

No Roses for Harry! by Gene Zion
Text copyright © 1958 by Eugene Zion
Reprinted by permission of HarperCollins Publishers

Materials needed:
Underwater Friends

1. a. Listen as your teacher reads the literature passage. Copy the sentences. Compare your copy to the model and make corrections.

   b. Discuss the literature passage with your teacher.

      1) *Harry was unhappy about his sweater. People and dogs were making fun of him. Harry made a decision to do something. What was Harry trying to do?*
      2) *What has happened to Harry's plan so far?*

1) lose his sweater
2) Each time someone returned it.

   c. When we want to tell the order in which things happen, we number them. To number something, we can use numbers 1, 2, 3, 4, or we can use words first, second, third, fourth. Underline the number order word in our sentences.

c. first

   d. Orally, tell your teacher four things that happened to Harry in our passage, in the correct order, using number order words to tell how things happened.

   e. Copy the spelling words from Focus on Spelling:
      lose   found   lady   then.

d. First, he tried to lose it in the pet department. Second, a man found it and gave it back. Third, he tried to lose it in the grocery department. Fourth, a lady found it and gave it back.

2. a. In the literature passage, Harry went to a big department store. What is a department store? What are some department stores in your area?

   b. There are two settings, or scenes, in the passage. One is in the pet department, and one is in the grocery department. Draw a picture showing what it may have looked like in each department with Harry there. Include things that would be in that department.

c. We have learned many things about Harry. Write or dictate a story about an adventure that Harry might have.

d. See-Spell-Say
Look and **see** each word in the spelling list. **Spell** the word aloud. **Say** the word.

3.
a. (Date) May 10, 1998
(Greeting) Dear Ann,

(Body) I was happy to see you at the store. Please come to my house to play soon. I have a new dog.

(Closing) Your friend,
(Signature) Sue

3. a. Here is an example of a friendly letter.

> May 10, 1998 *(Date)*
> Dear Ann, *(Greeting)*
>
>   I was happy to see you at the store. Please come to my house to play soon. I have a new dog. *(Body)*
>
>   Your friend, *(Closing)*
>   Sue *(Signature)*

Locate these parts in our sample letter: *date, greeting, body, closing, and signature* and label them.

✐ Teacher's Note: If your student would like to find out what happened at the end of the story, check this book out from the library. See how his advice compares to what Harry really did.

b. We have read about Harry's struggles, and now it is time for us to give Harry some advice, or tell him what we think will be the best thing for him to do.

Write Harry a letter, suggesting how he should take care of this problem.

Include all the parts of a letter. Indent (or move in about half an inch from the left hand margin) the paragraph.

c. Spelling Words Puzzle

c. 1) then
2) found
3) lose
4) lady

4. a. Find the story "A Barn for Seahorse" and read it to your teacher.

b. Discuss the story with your student:

1) *Tell me the story in your own words.*
2) *Why did Seahorse have trouble making his barn at the beginning of the story?*
3) *What happened that changed Seahorse's situation?*
4) *How did this help Seahorse complete his job?*

c. Every story has three parts, the beginning, the middle, and the end. Describe what is happening in each picture. On the lines beside the picture, write two sentences about the picture.

Ask your teacher to help you edit the sentences. When this is completed, read all the sentences to your teacher. Color the pictures and share the story with someone.

d. Look at the word: *picture*. The letters **ture** in this word is pronounced **/cher/**.

Read the words in the Phonics Word Box to your teacher: *nature picture vulture lecture*.

e. Review your spelling words orally.

5. a. Review any words from the story "A Barn for Seahorse" that you have had difficulty reading.

b. Read the story aloud. Then mark the Reading Chart for that story.

c. Find page 329 in the *Student Activity Book*. Discuss what is seen in each picture.

1) *What do you think happened before each picture?*
2) *What do you think happened after each picture?*
3) *Who might the people be in the pictures?*

Write a story about one of the pictures. Spend plenty of time discussing the story with your teacher before anything is written. Be sure you have a beginning, middle, and end to the story. You may want to name the characters, if desired.

4.
b. 1) Answers will vary.
2) He did not have enough hands to hold everything.
3) Octopus helped him.
4) Octopus had enough hands to get the job done.

Use three pieces of paper when you are ready to write or dictate to your teacher. On the first one, write what happens at the beginning of the story. On the second one, write what happened in the middle of the story. On the third one, write what happened at the end of the story.

Cut out each picture and glue it in the appropriate place in the story. Staple the pages together and make a cover for the story.

d. Copy the literature passage using your best handwriting.

e. Optional: Spelling test

Rain

The rain is raining all around,
It falls on field and tree.
It rains on the umbrellas here,
And on the ships at sea.

Robert Louis Stevenson

1. a. Listen as your teacher reads the literature passage. Copy the sentences. Compare your copy to the model and make corrections.

   b. The poem in the literature passage says that it is raining all around. Find four places or things that it is raining on and underline them.

   c. When it rains, it does seem to be everywhere. How does a rainy day make you feel? Write or dictate a list of things you can do on a rainy day.

   d. Copy the spelling words from Focus on Spelling:
   rain   sea   tree   around.

2. a. We have learned about words that are names of people, places or things. These words are called nouns, or naming words. There are some little words that can come before namingwords that tell us a naming word is coming. Look for the word *rain* in the first line of our poem. *Rain* is a naming word, or noun. Underline the little word that comes before the word *rain*.

   b. The little word *the* tells us that a naming word will be next.

   Look at the rest of the poem and underline the word *the*. What does it tell us is coming? Circle the naming word that comes next.

✐ Teacher's Note: Poetry lines are often capitalized, although they do not necessarily begin a new sentence.

Materials needed:
Underwater Friends

1.
b. It is raining on fields, trees, umbrellas, and ships at sea.

✐ Teacher's Note: We will not define them as articles at this point. Sometimes, modifiers come between the article and noun.

2.
b. the umbrellas
the ships

2.

c. 1) Mom gave us (a) snack.

2) (The) dog likes to run and play.

3) I want to go to (the) park.

4) Where is (the) book?

5) We are going to (the) store.

6) Dad wants to take (a) picture.

3.

a. 1) I like to eat cake <u>and</u> ice cream.

2) Bobby likes peanut butter <u>and</u> jelly sandwiches.

3) It was cold <u>and</u> rainy today.

4) Mom likes to fix chicken <u>and</u> rice for dinner.

---

c. The word *a* is also a word that tells us a naming word is coming next. Read these sentences to your teacher and circle the words that tell a naming word is coming next.

1) Mom gave us a snack.
2) The dog likes to run and play.
3) I want to go to the park.
4) Where is the book?
5) We are going to the store.
6) Dad wants to take a picture.

d. Sometimes it seems that rain isn't a very fun thing, especially when it makes us stay inside. Rain is important though, so let's write a paragraph of three or four sentences. Remember to indent the first line of the paragraph. Write about the good things of rain. Draw a picture of some of these good results of rain. I'll give you one to start with - a beautiful rainbow! Discuss your thoughts with your teacher to help you get started.

e. See-Spell-Say
Look and **see** each word from the spelling list. **Spell** the word aloud. **Say** the word.

3. a. Read the second line of the poem aloud. This line tells us that the rain fell on field *and* tree. The word *and* connects or joins the two words, *field* and *tree*. Read the following sentences, find the connecting word and underline it.

1) I like to eat cake and ice cream.
2) Bobby likes peanut butter and jelly sandwiches.
3) It was cold and rainy today.
4) Mom likes to fix chicken and rice for dinner.

b. Trees and fields are a beautiful part of God's creation. No matter where we live, there is always some part of nature we can enjoy. Go on a nature walk with your teacher. The walk doesn't have to be long, just look around and see what aspects of nature you can enjoy. You may want to take a small bag with you and collect small pebbles, leaves, feathers, etc.

c. After your walk, talk with your teacher about what you saw and heard. Draw a picture, or pictures, of things you liked on a blank piece of paper. With your teacher's help, write descriptions of what you saw on the back of your drawings.

d. Find a field guide at your library or bookstore. Try to identify the objects you brought back from your nature hike. This may be the start of a new hobby.

e. Spelling Words Puzzle

4. a. Find the story, "Keep It Up," and read it to your teacher.

b. Discuss the story with your teacher:

1) *Tell me the story in your own words.*
2) *What did Tuna want to learn to do in this story?*
3) *How did Octopus help her?*
4) *How did Seahorse help her?*
5) *How did Lobster help her?*
6) *How are you like Tuna? How are you different from Tuna?*

c. Find page 337 in the *Student Activity Book*. There are several pictures of the characters and objects from the reader, *Underwater Friends*. Discuss these project ideas with your teacher and choose a project to work on today and tomorrow.

1) Color and cut out pictures. Use a shoe box and create a 3-D scene, or diorama, of the reef. Write or dictate a summary of a few stories from the reader or make up your own.

2) Color and cut out pictures. Create a sentence about six of the pictures. Glue each picture on the top of a paper and write the sentence under each picture.

3) Create a new story about our sea friends. Color and cut out the pictures. Make a book by stapling several pages together. Write the story in the book, and glue the pictures in as desired.

3.
e. 1) sea
2) rain
3) around
4) tree

4.
b. 2) juggle
3) He told her to swim in a straight line.
4) He told her to try two shells first.
5) He told her she was doing it correctly and needed to just keep practicing.

✍ **Teacher's Note:** If your student has not made a diorama yet, this would be a good time to do it. The sea creatures can be hung from the top of the box with string and the coral glued to the bottom. You may want to paint the inside of the box before you begin.

d. The letter combination **ch** usually says **/ch/** as in *each*. Sometimes **ch** says **/k/** as in *ache*.

Read the words in the Phonics Word Box to your teacher: *school   stomach   choir   Christmas   character*.

e. Review your spelling words orally.

5. a. Review any words from the story that you have had difficulty reading.

b. Read the story aloud. Then mark the Reading Chart for that story. You have now completed the book, *Underwater Friends*. Cut out the book cover and add it to your Reading Chart.

c. Complete your *Underwater Friends* project and prepare to present it to a group.

d. Copy the literature passage using your best handwriting.

e. Optional: Spelling test

1. a. Listen to your teacher as she reads the following poem:

The Swing

How do you like to go up in a swing,
Up in the air so blue?
Oh, I do think it the pleasantest thing
Ever a child can do!

Up in the air and over the wall,
Till I can see so wide,
River and trees and cattle and all
Over the countryside.

Till I look down on the garden green,
Down on the roof so brown.
Up in the air I go flying again,
Up in the air and down!

b. Discuss the poem with your teacher:

   1) *Tell me about this poem in your own words.*
   2) *Have you ever had a ride on a swing like this one? Tell me about it.*
   3) *What can the person in the poem see as he swings so high?*
   4) *How does the house look to him from the high swing? Why?*

c. On a separate piece of paper, copy the first verse of *The Swing,* beginning half way down the paper.

d. If you have a poetry book available, find illustrations for several poems. Illustrations usually show a part of the poem and are often colorful and fun. Draw a picture about the poem you wrote on the top part of your paper.

e. Find other poems about fun and play in your poetry book and read them with your teacher.

✐ Teacher's Note: This week you and your student will work on poetry. There is no reader for this lesson. Find portions of poems your student is easily capable of reading aloud, to continue this important fluency stage of reading.

✐ Teacher's Note: During this lesson, your student will make a poetry book. Please give him a folder to keep his papers together. He will make a book on the last day. As an option, you may want to find a general poetry book to use in this lesson.

1.
b. 3) river, trees, cattle, garden, roof
   4) He sees only the roof because he is looking down on the house from up high.

If you can take your student to a swing, ask him to swing as high as he can and tell you what he sees from up there.

2. a. Listen as your teacher reads the following poem:

Tired Tim

Poor tired Tim! It's sad for him.
He lags the long bright morning through,
Ever so tired of nothing to do;
He moons and mopes the livelong day,
Nothing to think about, nothing to say;
Up to bed with his candle to creep,
Too tired to yawn, too tired to sleep:
Poor tired Tim! It's sad for him.

Walter de la Mare

b. Discuss the poem with your teacher:

1) *Tell me about this poem in your own words.*
2) *Have you ever felt like Tired Tim? Tell me about it.*
3) *Why do you think Tim felt tired all the time?*
4) *Do you have any advice for him?*

c. On a separate piece of paper, copy any two lines of *Tired Tim*, beginning half way down the paper.

d. Illustrate the two lines at the top of the paper.

e. Find other poems about funny people or poems written by Walter de la Mare in your poetry book. Read them aloud with your teacher.

3. a. Listen as your teacher reads the following poem:

Celery

Celery, raw,
Develops the jaw,
But celery stewed,
Is more quietly chewed.

Ogden Nash

✏ **Teacher's Note: If possible, give your student a stalk of raw celery and ask him to eat some of it.**

b. Discuss the poem with your teacher:

    1) *Tell me about this poem in your own words.*
    2) *What does he mean by "develops the jaw"?*
    3) *Why does he talk about stewed celery as "quietly chewed?"*

c. Listen to your teacher as she reads the following poem:

The Kitten

The trouble with a kitten is
THAT
Eventually it becomes a
CAT.

           Ogden Nash

d. Discuss the poem with your teacher:

    1) *Tell me about this poem in your own words.*
    2) *Have you ever had a kitten as a pet? Tell me about it.*
    3) *How would you describe a kitten? How would you describe a cat?*
    4) *What does the author mean when he says the "trouble" with a kitten?*
    5) *Why do you think the words* that *and* cat *are written in all capital letters in this poem?*

e. On a separate piece of paper, copy one of the Ogden Nash poems, beginning half way down the paper.

f. Ask your student to illustrate the verse at the top of the paper.

g. Find other poems about animals or other poems written by Ogden Nash in your poetry book. Read them aloud with your teacher.

3
d. 5) to add to the rhyme and humor; for emphasis

✏ **Teacher's Note:**
The plural of fish may be written *fish* or *fishes*.

4.
b. 3) They shine in the sun.
   4) He looks like he is smiling when he opens his mouth.
   5) Alice in Wonderland

4. a. Read the following poem to your student:

How Doth the Little Crocodile

How doth the little crocodile
Improve his shining tail,
And pour the waters of the Nile
On every golden scale!

How cheerfully he seems to grin,
How neatly spreads his claws,
And welcomes little fishes in
With gently smiling jaws!

Lewis Carroll

b. Discuss the poem with your student:

1) *Tell me about this poem in your own words.*
2) *Have you ever seen a real crocodile? Tell me about it.*
3) *Why do you think the author calls his scales "golden"?*
4) *Why do you think the author calls his jaws "smiling"?*
5) *Have you ever heard of the author, Lewis Carroll? Do you know something else he wrote?*

c. On a separate piece of paper, copy the first verse of *How Doth the Little Crocodile,* beginning half way down the paper.

d. Illustrate the verse at the top of the paper.

e. Find other poems about animals or other poems by Lewis Carroll in your poetry book. Read them aloud with your teacher.

5. a. Listen as your teacher reads the following poem.

My Shadow

I have a little shadow that goes in and out with me,
And what can be the use of him is more than I can see.
He is very, very like me from the heels up to the head;
And I see him jump before me, when I jump into my bed.

The funniest thing about him is the way he likes to grow—
Not at all like proper children, which is always very slow;
For he sometimes shoots up taller like an India-rubber ball,
And he sometimes gets so little that there's none of him at all.

Robert Lewis Stevenson

b. Discuss the poem with your teacher:

   1) *Tell me about this poem in your own words.*
   2) *Have you ever seen your shadow? Tell me about it.*
   3) *What does the author mean when he says "I see him jump before me, when I jump into my bed"?*
   4) *What does the author mean in the last two lines of the poem?*

c. On a separate piece of paper, copy one or two lines from *My Shadow,* beginning half way down the paper.

d. Illustrate the lines at the top of the paper.

e. Find other funny poems in your poetry book. Read them aloud with your teacher.

f. Today, complete *Assessment 6* with your teacher.

5.
b. 3) The lamp next to the bed makes the shadow on the bed as the child gets into it.
  4) The shadow is long sometimes and short sometimes. It depends on the angle of the sun.

✎ Teacher's Note: Go outside sometime soon so your student can experiment with his shadow.

Assessment 6
(Lessons 26 - 31)

Assessment 6 is a written assessment. Find page 343 in the Student Activity Book. Ask him to complete it as you instruct him.

1. *Add **-ed** to the end of these words. Remember to change the **y** to **i** and add **ed**.*

   a. try _____   c. fry _____
   b. carry _____   d. hurry _____

2. *Adjectives are words that describe a noun, or naming word. Complete the sentences with an adjective.*

   a. *Justin saw a _____ dog.*
   b. *I will wear my _____ coat.*

3. *Pronouns are words that take the place of nouns. Underline the pronouns.*

   a. *Marcy brought her sister.*
   b. *Mom and Dad enjoyed their dinner.*

4. *Antonyms are words of opposite meaning. Draw lines to the matching antonym.*

   a. dark   break
   b. late   clean
   c. dirty   early
   d. fix   light

5. *Synonyms are words of similar meaning. Draw lines to the matching synonym.*

   a. messy   hear
   b. correct   untidy
   c. listen   kind
   d. nice   right

1. a. tried
   b. carried
   c. fried
   d. hurried

2.
a. Possible answers: big, brown, cute
b. Possible answers: blue, new, favorite

3.
a. Marcy brought <u>her</u> sister.
b. Mom and Dad enjoyed <u>their</u> dinner.

4.
   a. dark   break
   b. late   clean
   c. dirty   early
   d. fix   light

5.
   a. messy   hear
   b. correct   untidy
   c. listen   kind
   d. nice   right

Abraham Lincoln was born on a farm in the state of Kentucky on February 12, 1809.

Abraham Lincoln by Clara Ingram Judson.
Copyright © 1961 by Clara Ingram Judson.
Reprinted by permission of Modern Curriculum Press, Inc.

1. a. Listen as your teacher reads the literature passage. Copy the sentence. Compare your copy with the model and make corrections.

    b. This literature passage tells us about a very famous American. Underline the person's name in this sentence. *Do you know what important job he did for our country?*

    c. There are two facts about Abraham Lincoln in this passage. Read them to your teacher.

    d. A noun is the name of a person, place, or thing. In our passage there are several nouns. Find them and read them aloud.

    Look at the nouns, *state* and *Kentucky*. Can you tell the difference between these two nouns? The word *state* is called a **common noun**. It could be any state. The word *Kentucky* is a **proper noun**, it is the same of a particular state. All proper nouns are capitalized.

    Circle all the common nouns and underline all the proper nouns.

    e. Copy the spelling words from Focus on Spelling:
    born   farm   state   every.

2. a. In the literature passage, one of the important facts we learned about Abraham Lincoln was his birth date. Copy the date of his birth in our sentence. Tell your teacher three things about how the date is written.

    b. When we write a date, we write the name of the month, beginning with a capital letter, the day in the month, and the year. We separate the day of the month and the year with a comma. Why do you think the comma is put there?

✎ Teacher's Note:
One of the purposes of the next four lessons is to further acquaint the student with the life of Abraham Lincoln. Reading library books, the encyclopedia, or viewing tapes about him all contribute to this knowledge. In each of the next lessons, the student will be asked to share newly gained information about Lincoln's life; either in writing, orally, through pictures, or drama.

Materials needed:
Famous People

1.
b. Abraham Lincoln was one of the presidents of the United States.

c. 1) Lincoln was born in Kentucky.
   2) Lincoln was born on February 12, 1809.

d. <u>Abraham Lincoln</u>, (farm), (state), <u>Kentucky</u>, <u>February</u>

2.
a. Here are a few hints: First letter of the month, order of month, day and year, or a comma.

b. So all the numbers do not run together.

Practice writing today's date correctly, including the day, month, and year. Write your birthday, including the year you were born. For the remainder of this week, write the date on your daily work.

c. Look through favorite books and find proper nouns. Fill in the columns with proper nouns.

d. See-Spell-Say
Look and **see** each word in the spelling list. **Spell** the word aloud. **Say** the word.

3. a. Today's date is_____.

Children enjoy being told about their birth, and the events surrounding it. Find out about the day you were born. Use photos, baby books, or any other special keepsakes that has information. In what city and state were you born?

b. Write the date and place you were born. Also, write a few sentences telling something about the day you were born.

c. Call or write grandparents, aunts, or uncles and ask about their birthplaces, homes, and childhood memories. Write down whom you talked to, what you found out about, and write a few sentences about what you learned.

d. Spelling Words Puzzle

1) Your birthday is the day you were __ __ __ __.
2) __ __ __ __ __ girl wore red shorts.
3) South Carolina is the name of a __ __ __ __ __.
4) My uncle lives on a __ __ __ __.

4. a. Today's date is _____.

Find the story, "The Story Teller," in the reader, *Famous People*. Read it to your teacher.

b. Discuss the story with your teacher:

1) *Tell me about Hans Christian Andersen.*
2) *Why do you think he did not like school? Would you like it if you were he?*
3) *What did he enjoy as a child? Why do you think he did?*
4) *Do you know any of the stories that he wrote? Which ones?*

3.
d. 1) born
  2) Every
  3) state
  4) farm

4.
b. Some stories are:
"The Little Match Girl"
"The Ugly Duckling"
"The Emperor's New Clothes"
"The Little Mermaid"

c. Find the Story Folder for "The Emperor's New Clothes" on page 349 in the *Student Activity Book*. Listen to your teacher as she reads the story.

d. Discuss it with your teacher:

1) *Who are the characters in this story? Tell me about all of them.*
2) *What does the emperor think of the tailor? Why does he think that?*
3) *What is the tailor really doing to the emperor?*
4) *Why does everyone except the little girl pretend the Emperor is dressed in fine clothes?*

e. Prepare a production of *The Emperor's New Clothes*. This drama may be done with puppets or actors. On page 351 of the *Student Activity Book* you will find the puppets. If you choose to use actors, you will need to find costumes and props.

f. Review your spelling words orally.

5. a. Today's date is _____.

   Review any words from the story, "The Story Teller," that you have had difficulty reading.

b. Read the story aloud. Then mark the Reading Chart for that story.

c. Continue with your production and prepare to present it to a group.

d. Copy the literature passage using your best handwriting.

e. Optional: Spelling test

---

d.
1) emperor, messenger, tailor, servants, townspeople, little girl, girl's father, children Answers will vary.
2) The emperor thought the tailor was grand like himself because he looked wealthy and proud.
3) He is lying and cheating.
4) They did not want to appear foolish.

✎ Teacher's Note: If you use actors, you may want to make a paper bag for the emperor to wear instead of his underwear.

Teacher's Note:
There is a blank in the *Student Activity Book* for your student to write the date each day.

Materials needed:
Famous People

1.
b. 1) Abe learned about letters, numbers, and words.
2) Abe couldn't continue school because the teacher went away and he felt sad.
3) Abe was sad because he liked to learn.

Teacher's Note:
Be sure to emphasize that progress is the important part of learning.

Abe liked school. He learned letters and words. He learned to use numbers. But soon the teacher went away. There was no more school. Abe was sad.

Abraham Lincoln by Clara Ingram Judson.
Copyright © 1961 by Clara Ingram Judson.
Reprinted by permission of Modern Curriculum Press, Inc.

1. a. Listen as your teacher reads the literature passage. Copy the sentences. Compare your copy to the model and make corrections.

   b. Discuss the literature passage with your teacher.

      1) *When Abe, a shortened name for Abraham, was young, he went to school. Tell me three things Abe learned at school.*
      2) *Why couldn't Abe continue going to school? How did he feel about that?*
      3) *Why do you think Abe was sad about school ending?*

   c. Think of three subjects you learn in school. What are your favorite things to learn in those subjects?

   d. Copy the spelling words from Focus on Spelling:
      liked   school   teach   more.

2. a. Talk about the reasons for doing school and why you do it the way you do. While the grass may seem greener for some children at school, remind your student of the main purpose for any school — to learn.

   b. Think about some things you previously were unable to do but now can do as a result of time or teaching.

   c. Talk with your teacher about things you would like to learn about, or be able to do. Set some reasonable goals together with your teacher for learning these things. Choose at least one very specific skill or goal to work toward, such as reading a certain book or building or making something. Check your progress from time to time.

d. See-Spell-Say
Look and **see** each word on your Spelling List. **Spell** the word aloud. **Say** the word.

3. a. *Abe* is the name of a specific boy. *Abe* is called a proper noun. Circle the words that take the place of the name *Abe* in the second and third sentences of our passage. Since this word replaces a noun, it is called a pronoun.

b. The first sentence tells us something Abe did about school. Underline that word. *Liked* is an action verb, because it is something Abe does about school. Even though we cannot act it out, like *jump* or *hop*, it does show action.

c. Read the next two sentences of the literature passage and underline the action verb in each of them.

d. Spelling Words Puzzle

1) __ or __
2) l __ __ __ d
3) t __ __ ch
4) s __ __ oo __

4. a. Find the story, "The Plant Doctor," in the reader, *Famous People*. Read it to your teacher.

b. Discuss the story with your teacher:

1) *Tell me about George Washington Carver.*
2) *Why do you think Susan and Moses treated George like a son?*
3) *Why do you think the work of George Washington Carver is important?*
4) *Why do you think George spent his life helping others?*

c. There is a picture of George Carver with lines next to the picture. Find information about him in an encyclopedia or other reference books. Listen to your teacher as she reads sections of it. Discuss with your teacher some words that could describe the Plant Doctor. Now, write two to three sentences about George Washington Carver.

3.
a. He

b. liked

c. learned
learned

d. 1) more
2) liked
3) teach
4) school

4.
b. 3) He helped farmers use their land in a better way which meant more food and jobs for others.

c. Possible answers: curious, helpful, kind, hardworker George Carver worked hard. He was curious about the plant world, and he devoted his life to other people.

d. Review your spelling words orally.

5. a. Review any words from the story, "The Plant Doctor," that you have had difficulty reading.

b. Read the story aloud.

c. We have learned four ways to add the suffix **-ed** to a word.

   1) Just add **-ed**, as in *look - looked*.
   2) If the word ends with a short vowel and a consonant, double the consonant and add **-ed**, as in *hop - hopped*.
   3) If the word ends in a silent **e**, drop the **e** and add **-ed**, as in *smile - smiled*.
   4) If the word ends with a consonant and **y**, change the **y** to **i** and add **-ed**, as in *try - tried*.

Read the words in the Word Box with your teacher. Write each word adding **-ed** on the lines below the rule it follows.

bake	move	carry	marry
stop	arrive	fry	tap
invite	hug	jump	look
ask	cry	crash	mop

d. Copy the literature passage using your best handwriting.

e. Optional: Spelling test

5.
c. 1) Just add -ed --
jump, look, ask, crash
2) If the word ends with a short vowel and a consonant, double the consonant and add -ed -- stop, hug, mop, tap
3) If the word ends in a silent e, we drop the e and add -ed -- invite, arrive, bake, move
4) If the word ends with a consonant and y, change the y to i and add -ed -- carry, cry, marry, fry

At night Abe read by the light of the fire. His mother helped him with hard words, and he read all her books.

Abraham Lincoln by Clara Ingram Judson.
Copyright © 1961 by Clara Ingram Judson.
Reprinted by permission of Modern Curriculum Press, Inc.

1. a. Listen as your teacher reads the literature passage. Copy the sentences. Compare your copy to the model and make corrections.

   b. Discuss the passage with your teacher:

      1) *Do you think Abe wanted to learn? Why do you think that?*
      2) *How did Abe's mother help him learn?*
      3) *Is learning important to you? How can you show that you want to learn?*

   c. In the story, when the teacher went away, Abe found another way to learn. *How did his mother help him? How does your mother help you?* Write or dictate a list of the ways your mother or father help you learn.

   d. On a seperate piece of paper, write a letter to your teacher telling what you like about school. Give it to the teacher.

   e. Copy the spelling words from Focus on Spelling:
      night   read   fire   helped.

2. a. A noun is the name of a person, place, or thing. There are words we use that take the place of nouns. Here is an example of a word that takes the place of a noun:

   Mother is home.   *She* is home.

   Who is the person in the first sentence of our example? What word takes the place of Mother in the second sentence?

Materials needed:
Famous People

1.
b. 1) He read at night by firelight, which shows he wanted to learn.
   2) She helped him with hard words as he read.

✐ Teacher's Note: This writing is to be done by the student alone. Do not check it for spelling, punctuation, or proper grammar. Tell your student this if he is uncomfortable writing alone. It is for creativity and expression only.

2.
a. The word *she* is a pronoun because it takes the place of a noun, the word *Mother*.

2.

b. 1) (He) is at work. <u>Dad</u>

2) Josh gave the bike
to (him). <u>Bob</u>

3) (His) house is big.
<u>Tom</u>

4) Pick up (her) book.
<u>Sue</u>

c. His, him, he, her

✐ **Teacher's Note:**
This book is not the
same as the book
used for the literature
passage.

✐ **Teacher's Note:**
Due to the length of this
book, it is suggested
that you read to the
end of the page that
begins "In the meantime
Berry took care of the
store." A picture of
Abraham Lincoln and
Ann Rutledge is on the
opposite page. There
are no page numbers.

b. Read these sentences. After each pair of sentences, circle the pronoun in the second sentence. On the blank, write the word the pronoun replaces.

1) Dad is at work.   He is at work.
2) Josh gave the bike to Bob.   Josh gave the bike to him.
3) Tom's house is big.   His house is big.
4) Pick up Sue's book.   Pick up her book.

c. There are four pronouns in the literature passage. Find and underline them.

d. Find page 358 in the *Student Activity Book* and complete the activity for **2d** by completing each sentence with a noun, or naming word.

Read the sentences aloud.

e. See-Spell-Say
Look and **see** each word on your spelling list. **Spell** the word aloud. **Say** the word.

3. a. Read from the book, *Abraham Lincoln,* by Ingri and Edgar d'Aulaire.

b. Discuss the events of the story with your teacher. Talk with her about Abraham Lincoln's childhood, including the hardships and the good things, and his lifestyle.

c. Write or dictate a list of the things in Abe Lincoln's childhood.

d. The responsibilities that children are given have changed over the years. A pioneer boy like Abraham Lincoln would have more work to do than a boy today. Talk with your teacher, and make a list of the things a pioneer boy would have been asked to do.

e. Think of the kinds of things you are asked to do. Write or dictate these things.

Compare the two lists and point out ways they are similar and ways they are different.

f. Spelling Words Puzzle

It was a dark _____. I guess that is why the _____ seemed so bright. I watched my dad as he _____ the firemen connect the hose. The next day, we _____ about it in the newspaper.

4. a. Find the story, "The Special Teacher," and read it to or with your teacher.

b. Discuss the story with your teacher:

1) *Tell me about Anne Sullivan.*
2) *Why was it hard for Helen's parents to find a teacher for her?*
3) *Tell me some things that Anne Sullivan taught Helen.*
4) *Anne Sullivan was a special teacher. Can you think of two words to describe her?*

c. Anne Sullivan was a special teacher, and her student, Helen Keller, became a famous person. Spend time today with your teacher researching Helen Keller. Look for facts about her life in books and on the computer, interview grandparents and relatives who may know anything about her, visit a blind school, or watch the movie *The Miracle Worker*.

d. Report to your teacher or someone else, information you have learned about Helen Keller, in any fashion you desire.

e. Review your spelling words orally.

5. a. Review any words from the story, "The Special Teacher," that you have had difficulty reading.

b. Read the story aloud, then mark the Reading Chart for that story.

c. Review the four ways to add the suffix **-ing** to a word.

1) Just add **-ing**, as in *look - looking*.
2) If the word ends with a short vowel and a consonant, double the consonant and add **-ing**, as in *hop - hopping*.
3) If the word ends in a silent **e**, drop the **e** and add **-ing**, as in *smile - smiling*.
4) If the word ends with **y**, just add **-ing**, as in *try - trying*.

3.
f. night
fire
helped
read

4.
b. 2) She was blind and deaf and that made it difficult to teach her.
   3) to eat with a fork and spoon, read, and write
   4) possible answers: hard working, devoted, caring, loving

c. Helen Keller was born in 1880. Although deaf and blind, she learned to read, write, and speak. She graduated from Radcliffe in 1904. She devoted her life to blind people and their care. She was an author and lecturer until she died in 1968.

✐ Teacher's Note: Do not emphasize the presentation as much as the information learned on this project.

5.

c. Just add -ing:
hunting, washing,
cleaning, kicking

If the word ends with
a short vowel and a
consonant, double
the consonant and
add
-ing: clapping,
tagging, sitting,
running

If the word ends
in a silent e, drop
the e and add -ing:
shaking, giving,
baking, writing

If the word ends in y,
just add -ing: trying,
drying, marrying,
studying

Read the words in the Word Box with your student. Ask your student to copy each word under the correct column that tells how to add **-ing** to the word.

try	*dry*	*wash*	*clean*	*kick*	*clap*
marry	*study*	*run*	*shake*	*give*	*bake*
write	*hunt*	*tag*	*sit*		

d. Copy the literature passage using your best handwriting.

e. Optional: Spelling test

Now and then a teacher came to the school nearby. The children went when there was school. But Abe learned more at home.

Abraham Lincoln by Clara Ingram Judson.
Copyright © 1961 by Clara Ingram Judson.
Reprinted by permission of Modern Curriculum Press, Inc.

Materials needed:
Famous People

***Abraham Lincoln*
by Ingri and Edgar
d'Aulaire**

1. a. Listen as your teacher reads the literature passage. Copy the sentences. Compare your copy to the model and make corrections.

   b. Listen to your teacher as she reads the remainder of the book, *Abraham Lincoln*, by Ingri and Edgar d'Aulaire. Talk with your teacher about the issues and events discussed in the remainder of the book.

   c. Using a dictionary, look up these words with your teacher, discuss their meanings and how they related to Abraham Lincoln's life:

lawyer	senator	president
slavery	Civil War	

   d. Copy the spelling words from Focus on Spelling:
   came   near   went   home.

2. a. We can add the suffix **-ed** to the end of a verb, or doing word, to show that something has already happened. Find the word in our literature passage that ends with **-ed** and circle it.

   b. When a word ends with a silent **e,** we can drop the **e** and add **-ed**.
   Ex: hope + ed = hoped   love + ed = loved

   Add **-ed** to these words.
   1) smile   2) shine   3) invite   4) arrive

   Read the new words aloud, and write or dictate sentences using each of the new words.

2.
a. learned

2.
b. 1) smile - smiled
   2) shine - shined
   3) invite - invited
   4) arrive - arrived

217

2.

c. nouns

Possible answers:
1) dog - barked, ran, jumps
2) fish - swims, moves
3) horse - gallops, jumps
4) teacher - explains, corrects
5) boy - swims, runs
6) girl - sings, runs
7) baby - cried, smiles, crawls
8) bird - flew, sings, builds

3.

b. Correct Order

1809-Abraham Lincoln was born in Kentucky.
1818-Abraham Lincoln's mother died.
1830-The Lincoln family moved to Illinois.
1837-Lincoln moved to Springfield and became a lawyer.
1842-Lincoln and Mary Todd were married.
1846-Lincoln elected to U.S. House of Representatives
1860-Lincoln was elected president.
1861-The Civil War began.
1864-Lincoln was re-elected president.
1865-Abraham Lincoln died.

d. 1) went
  2) home
  3) near
  4) came

c. Read the following words. What types of words are these? Verbs are doing words. Write a verb that tells what the noun might do.

1) dog   2) fish   3) horse   4) teacher
5) boy   6) girl   7) baby   8) bird

Read your noun/verb phrases aloud. You may act some of them out or illustrate three of them.

d. See-Spell-Say
Look and **see** each word in your spelling list. **Spell** the word aloud. **Say** the word.

3. a. We have now completed our passages on Abraham Lincoln. Discuss with your teacher the information you have learned about Abraham Lincoln. Make a list of at least five facts, or true statements you know about him.

b. Tape two pieces of paper together to make a piece 22 inches long. Turn the paper horizontally, and draw a line across to make a timeline of Abe Lincoln's life. Make marks to show the years. Cut out the event strips found on page 367 of the *Student Activity Book* and glue the events in the proper place on the timeline. Ex:

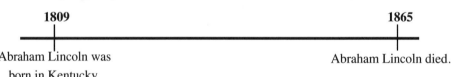

1809
Abraham Lincoln was
born in Kentucky.

1865
Abraham Lincoln died.

c. Discuss these options with your teacher and choose at least two of the following ways to present the information you have learned about Abraham Lincoln to others: in writing, orally, through drama, or illustrations. Invite someone to learn more about a great president.

d. Spelling Words Puzzle

4. a. Find the story, "The Famous General," and read it to or with your teacher.

b. Discuss the story with your teacher:

1) *Tell me about George Washington.*
2) *Why do you think Jack was scared to talk to George Washington? How would you feel if you were Jack?*
3) *How did you feel about George Washington as you read this story? Was he kind or proud?*
4) *Do you know anything else about him that is not in the story?*

c. When looking up a person in the encyclopedia, you look under the last name. In what letter volume would we find George Washington?

Look up George Washington in the encyclopedia or other reference book. Make a timeline or list character traits for him. You may use the picture of George Washington on page 367 of the *Student Activity Book*.

1732 - He was born on February 22nd, in Pope's Creek, Virginia.
1753 - He became the leader of the Virginia army.
1759 - He married Martha Custis.
1787 - He helped write the United States Constitution.
1789 - He was elected the first president of the United States.
1793 - He was elected a second term as president.
1797 - He retired to Mount Vernon.
1799 - George Washington died.

d. Review your spelling words orally.

5. a. Review any words from the story, "The Famous General," that you have had difficulty reading.

b. Read the story aloud, then mark the Reading Chart for that story.

c. Words can have similar meanings, called synonyms, such as *little* and *small*. Tell your teacher a synonym for each word you read: *big short correct*

4.
c. the W volume

5.

c. *big* - large, huge
short - small, little
correct - right, true

brave - scared, afraid
open - closed
healthy - sick, ill

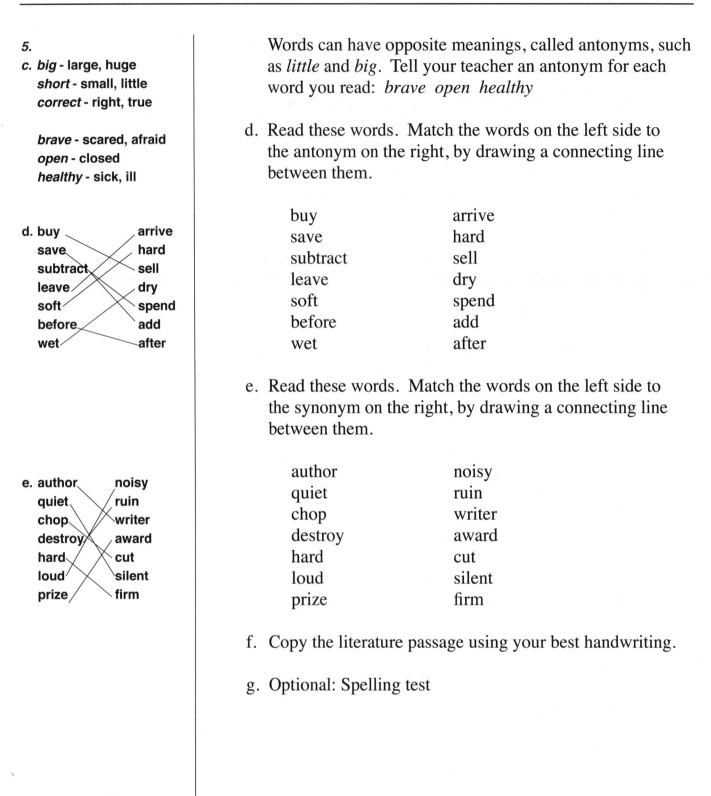

d. buy   arrive
  save   hard
  subtract   sell
  leave   dry
  soft   spend
  before   add
  wet   after

e. author   noisy
  quiet   ruin
  chop   writer
  destroy   award
  hard   cut
  loud   silent
  prize   firm

Words can have opposite meanings, called antonyms, such as *little* and *big*. Tell your teacher an antonym for each word you read: *brave open healthy*

d. Read these words. Match the words on the left side to the antonym on the right, by drawing a connecting line between them.

buy	arrive
save	hard
subtract	sell
leave	dry
soft	spend
before	add
wet	after

e. Read these words. Match the words on the left side to the synonym on the right, by drawing a connecting line between them.

author	noisy
quiet	ruin
chop	writer
destroy	award
hard	cut
loud	silent
prize	firm

f. Copy the literature passage using your best handwriting.

g. Optional: Spelling test

Little drops of water,
Little grains of sand,
Make the mighty ocean
And the pleasant land.

Mother Goose Rhyme

Teacher's Note:
Poetry lines are often capitalized, although they do not necessarily begin a new sentence.

Materials needed:
Famous People

1. a. Listen to your teacher as she reads the literature passage. Copy the sentences. Compare your copy to the model and make corrections.

   b. This passage is a beautiful description of the ocean and the land, and it tells how even big things are made up of small parts.

   On the bottom of a blank piece of paper, copy the phrase *The Mighty Ocean*. On the same piece of paper, draw pictures or cut pictures out of magazines to show what the phrase means.

   Do the same with *The Pleasant Land*.

   c. A noun names a person, place, or thing. An adjective is a word that describes a noun. Cut out the word cards for **1c** on page 373 of the *Student Activity Book*. Put all the noun word cards on the right side. Read the remaining cards and decide which adjective best describes each noun.

   Glue the cards in adjective / noun order on a blank piece of paper and illustrate three of the word combinations.

   d. Copy the spelling words from Focus on Spelling: *water   little   land   sand*.

2. a. We are going to look at adjectives, or examples of describing words before the name of an object:

   big truck   happy boy   sweet candy

   Look at the literature passage. Underline all the adjectives, or words that describe a noun.

c. adjectives - describing words nouns - naming words

   Possible answers:
   big dog
   tall boy
   happy family
   sweet cake
   brown pony

2.
a. **little, little, mighty, pleasant**

221

b. Discuss with your teacher what each of these adjectives, or describing words, means. Think of another person, place, or thing these underlined words can describe. Write or dictate a sentence using each describing word.

c. See-Spell-Say
Look and **see** each word on your spelling list. **Spell** the word aloud. **Say** the word.

3. a. Sometimes we put two words together to make a new word. This new word is called a compound word. Here's an example: seahorse

This compound word tells you about the object A seahorse is an animal that looks similar to a *horse* and lives in the *sea*.

Read these compound words to your student and ask him to tell you about the word. Ex: keyhole It is a *hole* that is made for a *key*.

bedroom	*rowboat*
farmhouse	*toothpaste*
beehive	

b. Find page 373 in the *Student Activity Book*, and cut out the word cards for **3b.** Match the two words that make a new compound word. Glue them on a blank piece of paper and illustrate three of the compound words.

c. Spelling Words Puzzle

1) I play in the _____ and _____ at the beach.
2) The opposite of *big* is _____.
3) The word _____ rhymes with band.

4. a. Find the story, "The Pioneer Girl," and read it to or with your teacher.

3.
a. bedroom - It is a room with a bed in it.

farmhouse - It is the house on a farm.

beehive - It is a hive made by bees.

rowboat - It is a boat you row.

toothpaste - It is paste made to clean your teeth.

b. raincoat   basketball
birdhouse   mailbox
bookstore   seashore

c. 1) water and sand
   2) little
   3) land

✐ **Teacher's Note:**
If your student is unfamiliar with the *Little House Series*, this is a good time to begin them. You may want to use them as read-alouds for the summer.

b. Discuss the story with your teacher:

1) *Tell me anything you know about Laura Ingalls Wilder.*
2) *Why are the girls worried about Pa? Would you be worried if you were Laura?*
3) *What happened to Laura and Mary's Christmas candy? How did they feel about that? How would you feel if you were Laura?*

c. Discuss the characters in "The Pioneer Girl" with your teacher: Laura, Mary, Pa, Ma. Quotation marks tell us that someone is speaking. The actual words that are spoken by each person are enclosed in quotation marks.

Assign these parts to two or three people. Ask the readers to practice saying these words with correct expression.

When everyone is ready, each person may read the parts with expression or act the story out with props and actions.

d. Review the spelling words orally.

5. a. Review any words from the story, "The Pioneer Girl," that you have had difficulty reading.

b. Read the story aloud. Then mark the Reading Chart for that story. You have now finished *Famous People*. Add the book cover to your Reading Chart.

c. Review the people you learned about in the reader, *Famous People*. Look at the pictures with your teacher and discuss the story and people in the story. If there is any person that you would like to know more about, spend some time at the library finding books on that person.

Look through the encyclopedia or other reference books and note different people who have impacted their world.

d. Think about the things that interest you.`

4.b.
1) Answers will vary.
2) There is a snowstorm and Pa is late coming home.
3) Pa ate it. The girls were glad Pa had the candy to eat.

✎ **Teacher's Note: Discuss them only as long as your student is interested.**

What are you curious about?
What character traits do you want in your life?
What do you really care about?
How do you want to spend your time?

Spend some time talking about these things. With your teacher, make a list of things you can do in the next months that will help you achieve these goals.

e. Copy the literature passage using your best handwriting.

f. Optional: Spelling test

g. Today, complete *Assessment 7* with your teacher.

✏ **Teacher's Note: If you are beginning a break from school, it may be a good time to think of a project for your student. The project could be a garden, care of an animal, a sewing project, reading about a subject or person, or collecting information on the family's history. Find books on the subject and encourage your student to enjoy the subject as he learns about it.**

If you have not read *The Little House* series to your student, this may be a good time to start.

Assessment 7
(Lessons 31 - 36)

1. *A common noun names any person, place, or thing. A proper noun names a particular person, place, or thing. Underline the common nouns, and circle the proper nouns.*

   a. The man knocked on the door.
   b. Jack looked out the window.

2. *Add **-ed** to these words.*

   a. wash
   b. poke
   c. marry
   d. tap

3. Add **-ing** to these words.

   a. hike
   b. spy
   c. bump
   d. pat

4. *Underline the actual words spoken.*

   "I lost my pencil," said Adam.

5. *Make three compound words using the word **every** and the following words: thing one day.*

1.
a. The <u>man</u> knocked on the <u>door</u>.
b. (Jack) looked out the <u>window</u>.

2.
a. washed
b. poked
c. married
d. tapped

3.
a. hiking
b. spying
c. bumping
d. patting

4. <u>I lost my pencil</u>

5. everything
   everyone
   everyday

Skills Index

Numbers beside each skill indicate lesson numbers.
* Indicates the skill is taught throughout the program.

Composition

address - 11
creative writing *
dates - 11, 32

descriptive writing - 2, 6, 9, 19, 21, 33
letter writing - 11, 19, 28, 29, 34

Creative Expression / Games

bingo 2
book making - 10, 15, 20, 30
calendar - 4
card making - 4, 8, 26
decorating hats - 19
diorama - 10, 15, 20, 30
drama - 2, 5, 35

illustrating *
interpreting illustrations - 5, 6, 8, 13, 14
leaf rubbing - 1
nature walk - 30
oral presentation - 4
pantomime - 9, 12
puppetry - 22

Grammar

Higher Order Thinking Skills

Phonics / Spelling

Reading

compound words - 1, 4, 8, 9, 13, 16, 17, 18, 21, 22, 24, 25,36
comprehension *
fact - 3, 12, 17, 35
fiction - 7
nonfiction - 7
opinion - 3, 12, 17
ordinal numbers - 24, 29
poetry - 3, 4, 12, 30, 31

poetry appreciation - 31
rhyme - 9
sentence - 14, 18, 20
summary - 15
syllable *

Research and Study Skills

atlas - 7, 11, 26
encyclopedia - 3, 26, 27, 35, 36
map skills - 5, 7, 11, 26
parts of a book - 10, 15, 27, 28
parts of a story - 25

survey - 3
thesaurus - 10, 28
timeline - 35

Additional Literature Used in Lessons

(listed in order of use)

A Tree is Nice by Janice May Udry. HarperCollins Publishers.

Little Bear by Else Holmelund Minarik. HarperCollins Publishers.

The Bravest Dog Ever by Natalie Standiford. Random House.

The Fire Cat by Esther Averill. HarperCollins Publishers.

Yonder by Tony Johnson. Dial Books.

The Ox-Cart Man by Donald Hall. Penguin Group.

Corduroy by Don Freeman. Penguin Group.

The Little Island by Golden MacDonald. Random House.

Billy and Blaze by C.W. Anderson. Simon & Schuster.

Harry the Dirty Dog by Gene Zion. HarperCollins Publishers.

Abraham Lincoln by Ingri and Edgar d'Aulaire. Beautiful Feet Books.

See where learning takes you.
www.commonsensepress.com

Congratulations,

You Are Part Of The *Common Sense Press* Family.

Now you can receive our FREE e-mail newsletter, containing:
- Teaching Tips
- Product Announcements
- Helpful Hints from Veteran Homeschoolers
- & Much More!

Please take a moment to register with us.

Common Sense Press
Product Registration
8786 Highway 21
Melrose, FL 32666

Or online at
www.commonsensepress.com/register

After registering, search our site for teaching tips, product information, and ways to get more from your *Common Sense Press* purchase.

Your Name _____

Your E-Mail Address _____

Your Address _____

City _____ State _____ Zip _____

Product Purchased _____

From What Company Did You Purchase This Product? _____

Get involved with the *Common Sense Press* community.
Visit our web site often to contribute your ideas, read how others
are teaching their children, see new teaching tips, and more.